WILLIAM WALTON : THE ROMANTIC LONER

A Centenary Portrait Album

Humphrey Burton & Maureen Murray

William Walton
The Romantic Loner

A Centenary Portrait Album

OXFORD

UNIVERSITY PRESS

Great Clarendon Street, Oxford OX2 6DP

Oxford University Press is a department of the University of Oxford.
It furthers the University's objective of excellence in research, scholarship,
and education by publishing worldwide in

Oxford New York

Athens Auckland Bangkok Bogotá Buenos Aires Cape Town
Chennai Dar es Salaam Delhi Florence Hong Kong Istanbul Karachi
Kolkata Kuala Lumpur Madrid Melbourne Mexico City Mumbai Nairobi
Paris São Paulo Shanghai Singapore Taipei Tokyo Toronto Warsaw

with associated companies in Berlin Ibadan

Oxford is a registered trade mark of Oxford University Press
in the UK and in certain other countries

Published in the United States
by Oxford University Press Inc., New York

British Library Cataloguing in Publication Data
Data available

Library of Congress Cataloging in Publication Data
Data available

ISBN 0–19–816235–9

10 9 8 7 6 5 4 3 2 1

Typeset by George Hammond Design
Printed in Great Britain
on acid-free paper by
Butler & Tanner Ltd,
Frome and London

CONTENTS

FOREWORD

WILLIAM WALTON'S MUSIC is inimitable, harmonically, rhythmically and melodically. There are relatively few composers of the twentieth century whose music is instantly recognisable; too many of them were caught in the maelstrom of fashionable international complications. But almost any given few bars or phrases of Walton's output can be identified as his and only his, by any listener of experience.

In his earlier work there is an intensity, a rage, or even (as actually dictated by him) malice, which sweeps the listener along in a kind of hurtling, downhill path. But even his violent music is ardent and personal and quite irresistible. The energy of his material was never knowingly and calculatedly manufactured, as were many of the motorised efforts of some of his colleagues; it seems rather to be an inevitable expression of his personality.

It has to be said that it is in the more extrovert romanticism that Walton's music truly excels. His melodies are ravishingly beautiful, the themes tend to be long and spun out and the atmosphere is both expressive and intimate. He was very fond of wide, yearning intervals and he used them, cloaked in his lush instrumentation, with consummate skill. He preferred the time-honoured structures of musical history: symphonies, overtures, sonatas, concertos and oratorios, and he stayed away from the self-conscious titles so beloved by the aggressively intellectual branch of his art.

He used to sit and listen to records of Bellini's operas with admiration filling his eyes. He was immensely successful all his life, but always self-deprecating about his place in English music. He was a consummate composer, his technique self-assured and fluid and his output enviable.

For more than two decades I had the privilege of his friendship, both musical and personal. He was unfailingly amusing, often quite ribald, and always kind and encouraging. It is one of the great pleasures of my life to have known him well.

SIR ANDRÉ PREVIN

AUTHORS' INTRODUCTION

AMONG THE FIRST 78s I bought as a boy (writes Humphrey Burton) was Frederick Riddle's interpretation of the Walton Viola Concerto, still my favourite recording of that mysterious work. As a teenager I felt an instant identification with Walton's music. I loved the heart-aching romance of the early concertos, the drama of *Belshazzar's Feast*, the turbulence and tensions of the First Symphony. Many years later I relished the tight-rope experience of narrating the poems of *Façade* and had the joy of working with my childhood idol as the director of several televised concerts and documentaries filmed at his home on Ischia. Visits to La Mortella were red-letter days, fuelled by Lady Walton's marvellous cooking and Walton's delight in delivering deadpan assessments of himself and his colleagues.

I met William Walton (writes Maureen Murray) when I had just landed my first job, working as the Production Secretary of Tony Palmer's documentary film *At the Haunted End of the Day*. Walton was elderly and frail, but dressed in a beautifully cut suit and although he was extremely ill he still had a twinkle behind the eyes that sliced through the age barrier. It's a quality which has stayed with me ever since – a sizing up, an appraising in one glance: how can this person be useful to me? – the mark of a real artist. After her husband's death, Lady Walton invited me to Ischia to help her organise material for her memoirs. That initial work laid the foundations of the Archive which I set up at her instigation in 1990 and which has grown ever since, rather like one of the trees in her tropical garden.

We met in that Archive and soon decided to make a book together in time for Walton's centenary. Although he was imbued with the English cathedral tradition, which stretches back to Tudor times, he was to become the beneficiary of many of the twentieth century's technical innovations that affected music: broadcasting, electrical recording, sound films, television, even video. Preparing our album, as we call it, has provided the opportunity to search out much new material which will give a sense not just of the ups and downs in Walton's creative life but also the times through which he lived.

The background we share in film and television no doubt prompted our picture-led approach to the biographer's task. You can dip into any section of the book as you wish, but we would prefer you to experience it in its essentially chronological form, each double page spread revealing another episode in

Walton's story. The chapters all begin with a brief essay highlighting the notable biographical events of the period and the composer's significant compositions. Then the images take over, illuminated by independent anecdotes and quotations from Walton's self-deprecating and trenchant interviews. Our sources are given at the end of the book together with a selected list of major works, which are indexed to show the various pages on which they are featured.

Every student of Walton must be especially indebted to three authors. Susana Walton, his widow, has been the proverbial tower of strength to both of us and her book of memoirs, *Behind the Façade*, is a prime source. Stewart Craggs is a unique personality in the landscape of British musical scholarship. His *Source Book* and *Annotated Catalogue* have been indispensable. "We turn to Craggs!" has been our cry a hundred times. And finally the biographer Michael Kennedy, whose *Portrait of Walton* remains a joy and an inspiration. We owe to him the title for our book: *The Romantic Loner*. The suggestion came in a hand-written postcard on which he had added the jocular note: "Loner, not Lover". It is surely correct to describe Walton as a loner because at so many crucial moments he went his own way. He ducked out of Oxford, turned down teaching jobs to strike out on his own as a composer and lived abroad whenever he could, away from the rat-race. Was he truly a "romantic" personality? Perhaps not, in the sense of a Wagner or a Berlioz, but his music pulsates with emotion and you only have to glance at the photographs of Walton in his twenties to see that he had a terrific sense of style.

At the conclusion of his biographical study Michael Kennedy wrote: "Walton the man remains an enigma. The assumed diffidence was a mask . . . his music too is an enigma because it does not tell us the whole truth about William Walton." Our modest hope is that these pages will help you to understand him a little better and enjoy his music to the full.

HUMPHREY BURTON & MAUREEN MURRAY

CHAPTER 1

THE OLDHAM CHILDHOOD

1902–1912

"It was very picturesque . . . outside loos . . . that sort of thing"

WALTON'S MEMORY OF HIS HOME TOWN

WILLIAM WALTON was born in Lancashire in the town of Oldham, which lies seven miles north-east of Manchester at the edge of the Pennines and adjacent to the West Riding of Yorkshire. Oldham was incorporated as a town in 1849 and enjoyed two booms of mill construction in the 1860s and 1870s. By the year of Walton's birth, 1902, it was the most important cotton-spinning centre in the world: a third boom in 1904 saw the number of mills increase to 281 and by the end of World War I there were 320 of them. These large, plain brick buildings, each with a tall chimney belching black smoke, gave the Oldham skyline its "satanic" character. They stood "cheek by jowl with dwellings, hotels, perhaps even churches, in a way that must be seen to be believed", wrote a local newspaper in 1908, when Walton was six. "Within a few yards of the town hall you can hear the low purring growl of caged machinery . . . The smoke of the innumerable tall chimneys lies over all like a poultice . . . Brick houses and shops go on for ever and at the back of them, blotting out all the rest of the world, rise great precipitous mills like frowning cliffs, at whose base are the small houses where the folks live like coneys at a mountain foot."

Workers in an Oldham cotton spinning factory.

The Walton family resided in a more salubrious part of the town, close to Werneth Park, but the mills were a daily part of young "Billie's" landscape. His father, Charles Walton, a singer, had been a late starter in his profession. Born in 1867, he was already 26 when his fine bass-baritone voice won him a place at the newly-established Royal Northern College of Music. As a student he sang the roles of Mephistopheles in Gounod's *Faust* and Papageno in Mozart's *The Magic Flute,* but the operatic career that seemed to be beckoning did not materialise and in later life he was bitter about his lack of success, apparently turning for solace to drink. His wife Louisa (Louie) Turner was also a singer and voice teacher: they were both already in their thirties when they married and moved to 93, Werneth Hall Road in Oldham. Charles had a clerical job at an iron works but by the time their first son Noel was born, in 1899, he was sufficiently well-established to describe himself on the birth certificate as a teacher of singing. He also taught in Glossop, Hyde and Manchester. In Oldham he was choirmaster and organist at St John's, Werneth, then one of the town's leading churches and now a carpet warehouse.

William, born March 29, 1902, joined his brother Noel among the choir's boy trebles, taking part in the Sunday morning services and the annual performances of great choral masterpieces such as *Messiah* and *The Creation*. A special musical talent was early in evidence: his mother reported he could sing phrases from *Messiah* before he could speak. His father was a stern disciplinarian: young Billie remembered that whenever he sang a wrong note he would be rapped over the knuckles. But the boy must also have enjoyed performing in public since he recalled "making a scene (tears etc.) because not allowed to sing a solo when about the age of six". His father tried him on the violin without success and he also learned the piano. He was always self-deprecating about his performing skill, but the boy Walton must have had a modicum of ability as a

Mr and Mrs Charles Walton
on their wedding day
in the town of their courtship:
Chorlton-cum-Hardy.

3

Top of the High Street, Oldham, 1906.

pianist: he later won a piano prize at Christ Church Choir School and he was only sixteen when he composed a virtuoso keyboard part for a piano quartet. Paradoxically he was later to write more sympathetically for the string instruments than the piano: not even Shostakovitch or Britten could match the sustained lyrical beauty of Walton's three great concertos for violin, viola and cello.

The scant reports of the boy Walton's early childhood provide few signposts concerning the future composer's psyche. He seems to have imbibed the great tradition of English choral music with his mother's milk, he sang in children's Sunday school groups, heard marching brass bands on parade in the Oldham streets during public fêtes such as the Whit Walks and the Wakes Week and experienced the arbitrary counterpoint of the fairground on holiday trips to the seaside at Blackpool and Lytham St Anne's. There would have been a piano at home since his parents both gave singing

lessons in the parlour, but there was nobody in Oldham, it seems, to encourage him to compose: the sights and sounds of his childhood were stored for a later awakening of his imagination. Aspects of his Lancashire upbringing never to be lost were the flat vowels of the local accent, a taste for Lancashire Hotpot and a certain canniness where money was concerned.

Walton later spoke disparagingly of his Oldham terrace house, complaining of its "outside loo", but that was standard building practice in those days in the north of England and the buildings are of pleasing exterior design with gardens at front and back. Walton seems to have been reasonably happy as a child. The family was not well off, however, and soon there were more mouths to feed: a sister, Nora, was born in 1908 and a younger brother, Alec, in 1910. School, when it came, was a nightmare. "My elder brother went to the grammar school", Walton reported, "but my father couldn't afford sending me there, too, so I was sent to the local [board] school round the corner, which was very rough."

Billie's future seemed unpromising but in 1912, when he was ten, his father saw a newspaper advertisement announcing voice trials at Oxford. He applied on Billie's behalf and an audition was arranged. Did Charles then get cold feet? On the night before the audition he went on a disastrous pub crawl. Perhaps his musical friends egged the proud father on to a premature celebration. Perhaps he had a subconscious desire to prevent the inevitable separation from his son. At all events he was in no fit state next morning to accompany Billie to Oxford. The audition was in jeopardy. One can imagine the humiliation Louie Walton must have felt when she discovered that the money for the tickets had all been spent on booze. She took over decisively. Cash had to be borrowed from the greengrocer. The boy was very sick during the long journey and by the time he and his mother reached Oxford the auditions had finished. He burst into tears but Mrs Walton

persuaded the organist Dr Henry Ley to let him have a go. "I sang a few tests, which was all new to me," Walton remembered, "and then sang what I had prepared, a thing by Marcello" – it was the aria *O Lord our Governor*.

William Turner Walton was accepted and duly left home to become a probationary member of Christ Church Cathedral School, one of the world of sacred music's most revered institutions; the chapel of Christ Church College is also cathedral to the city of Oxford.

Brief visits home in the holidays enabled Charles to continue his son's general education in music. At what was quite likely the very first concert he attended he had heard the *Nutcracker Suite* by Tchaikovsky, played by the Oldham Orchestral Society, and in 1916 and 1917 father and son went into Manchester to hear *Boris Godounov* and *Le Coq d'Or* at Sir Thomas Beecham's opera seasons. But for the next decade Walton's everyday life was to be watched over by surrogate parents: Oldham had lost him for ever.

A bevy of Edwardian beauties welcomes you to Oldham.

Charles Walton, Walton's father (1867–1924), was the son of an Inland Revenue official. Walton maintained that his father would have enjoyed a national reputation as a singer, had he survived into the age of broadcasting.

Louie Turner, William's mother (1866–1954). Her father was an excise man from Hull, but the family were known as upholsterers. Family tradition had it that the Turner workshop was commissioned by the Prince Consort to make furniture for Buckingham Palace.

The Turner family tree (above) and the assembled Turner and Walton families. Mr and Mrs Charles Walton were married on 10 August 1898.

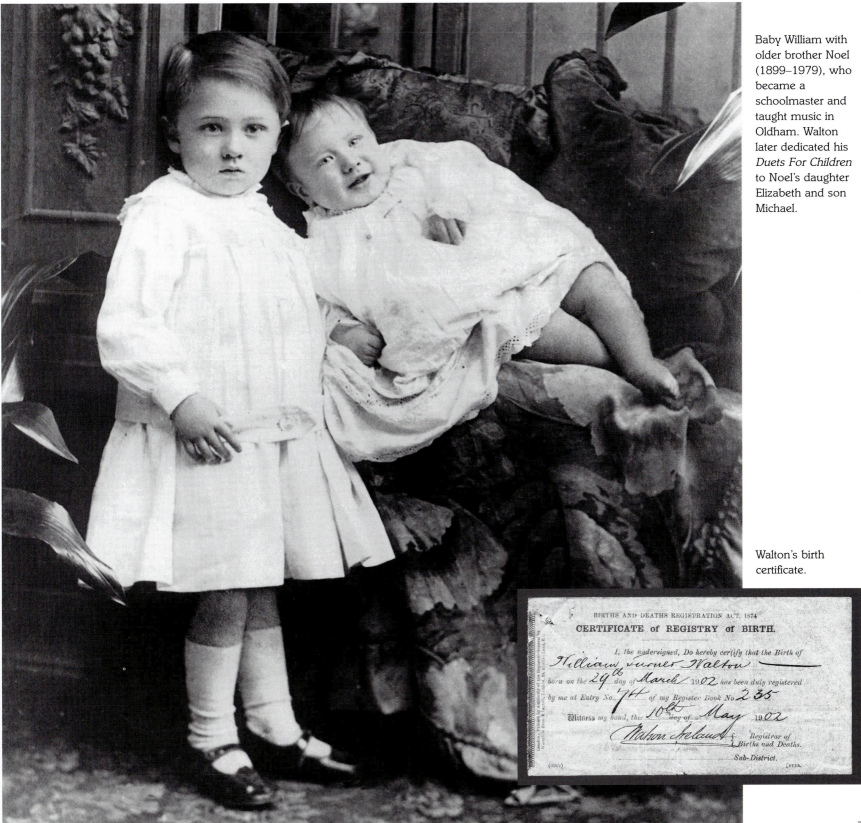

Baby William with older brother Noel (1899–1979), who became a schoolmaster and taught music in Oldham. Walton later dedicated his *Duets For Children* to Noel's daughter Elizabeth and son Michael.

Walton's birth certificate.

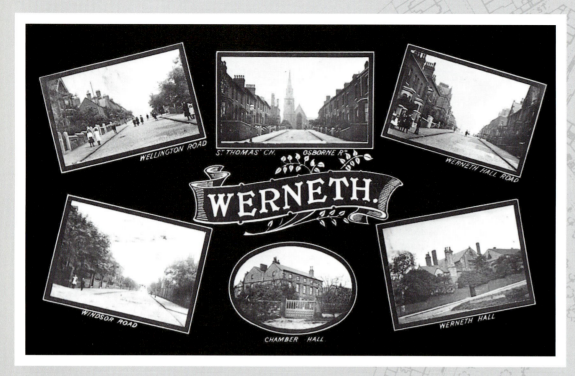

Postcard views of the young William's haunts in the Werneth district of Oldham.

Hartford New Works, where Charles Walton served as an office clerk when he and Louie first settled in Oldham. At the time of William's birth there were 270 cotton mills in Oldham, containing about twelve and a half million spindles and 18,000 looms. These mills accounted for a quarter of the cotton imported into the country.

Noel and William (encircled bottom left) outside the family home at 93 Werneth Hall Road. The road was on a steep hill leading down to the main road. William's favourite game was to put his little sister Nora on a tea tray and send her skidding down the incline. The trick was to run and overtake the tray before it and she were trampled underfoot by the busy horse and cart traffic on the Manchester Road.

Map of the Werneth district, 1902.

Interior, St John's Church, Werneth.

Young William's school. He remembered that "the boys were separated from the girls by iron railings; a pity". But undeterred, Walton stole his first kiss. "Her name was Elsie Slight."

WERNETH BOARD SCHOOL. F. & G. POLLARD 13, UNION STREET.

Noel and William sang in the choir at St John's Church. Noel lived in Oldham all his life. His pupils still remember his piano lessons with great affection. According to Walton's widow, Noel took up the composition of serial music when he retired "because he had nothing better to do".

St John's Church, Werneth.

All the fun of the fair during Oldham Wakes, the annual holiday period in northern England.

Noel and William in 1907.

*"What are you staring at, mariner man
Wrinkled as sea-sand and old as the sea?"*

From *Façade* by Edith Sitwell. Walton's settings of her poems became his first popular success.

Excursions during Oldham Wakes.

FAST EXCURSION TO BLACKPOOL and LYTHAM.

T. GREEN & CO.,
TEAMEN,
5, HIGH-ST., OLDHAM,

BLACKPOOL
AND
LYTHAM

ON OLDHAM WAKES TUESDAY.

PURCHASERS OF

4 lbs. of TEA will be PRESENTED with a RETURN TICKET
To EITHER OF THE ABOVE WELL-KNOWN WATERING PLACES.

TICKETS will be OFFERED TO THE PUBLIC at 2/9 EACH.

Holders of 16 Quarter-pound Tea Cheques will be PRESENTED with a
RAILWAY TICKET in return for their Cheques.

Persons going by T. GREEN & CO.'S TRIP will be Presented with Tickets for the
LAKES HALL GARDENS, WINTER GARDENS, and AQUARIUM, entitling holders
to admission on payment of FOURPENCE at each place, instead of Sixpence; and by
showing Railway Ticket at the NORTH PIER they will be admitted for ONE PENNY,
instead of Twopence, thereby effecting a saving of SEVENPENCE.

T. GREEN & CO. WILL GIVE

SPECIAL PRESENTS of Extraordinary for the WAKES!
Value

See our Windows at our ONLY Address, 5, HIGH STREET, OLDHAM.

10

My dear mother I hope
that you are keeping well
I suppose Nora and baby
will miss me. Noel is
rather glad I am away.
I am having a nice
time. Noel is going to
buy me a bagpipe
I last ball in the
winter garden.
With love from
Billie

"Billie"'s first surviving letter to his
mother (1910). He was eight years old.
A huntsman "playing on his old
bagpipe" appears in "Scotch Rhapsody"
from *Façade*.

"I do like to be beside the seaside . . .". Walton worked the tune of this popular song into the "Tango-Pasodoble" of *Façade*. He was soon faced with the threat of copyright infringement by the tune's legitimate publishers. But Walton resourcefully averted disaster (the tune did not come out of copyright until 1969) and came to a suitable accommodation about the "borrowed" phrase.

Blackpool Station. (left) The Oldham-born artist Helen Bradley was a contemporary of Walton. The families knew each other well and Bradley often saw young Billie running between their houses with armfuls of music sheets, desperately trying to avoid the puddles.

"The Beautiful Oldham Society" was born in the same year as Walton. Its credo: "We believe in the power of life to change the environment of life. The smoke-blackened walls and tall chimneys duly crumble and convey themselves away before the forces that lie dormant in the pale and wistful face of a little child."

The annual Flower Show at Werneth Hall, five minutes' walk down the hill from Walton's home. Perhaps young William was among the crowd gathered here in 1910.

"I could never organise my fingers properly." Yet Walton's own transcription for piano of the Waltz from *Façade* calls for virtuosity of the highest order.

Whit Walks by Helen Bradley. Walton's most spectacular excursion into the world of brass band music occurs in *Belshazzar's Feast*; two separate brass groups are employed to dramatic effect. Towards the end of his life Walton rescored his early ballet *The First Shoot* for the Grimethorpe Colliery Band.

Fancy dress cycle parade, Oldham, 1908. In his twenties Walton donned fancy dress with his friends for a Cecil Beaton home movie. In later years he designed his own clothes.

A magnet for small boys: Mr Granelli's ice cream cart. An early taste of Italy for young Billie.

Walton's earliest orchestral memory: *The Nutcracker Suite*. "I have never lost my affection for it." It was performed by the Oldham Orchestral Society in February 1912.

The Oldham Orchestral Society under the baton of William Lawton in the large hall of the Greenacres Co-operative Society Ltd, Oldham. "The society has been very successful in its efforts to promote concerts of a high standard." Lawton and Walton's father were good friends.

14

The Manchester Free Trade Hall, where Walton's father took him to concerts in his teens.

"BORIS GODOUNOV"

Music Drama in Three Acts and Seven Tableaux (after Pouchkine and Karamzine)

By M. P. MOUSSORGSKY.

CAST.		SYNOPSIS OF SCENERY.	
Boris	AUGUSTE BOUILLIEZ		
Feodor	ETHEL TOMS	**ACT I.**	
Xenia	D. ELLINGER	First Tableau	The Monastery of Novo-Dievitch
A Nurse	EDITH CLEGG	Second Tableau ...	The I
Chuisky	MAURICE D'OISLY	Third Tableau... ...	The Coronat
Pimène	POWELL EDWARDS	**ACT II.**	
Grigori	FREDERICK BLAMEY	Fourth Tableau ...	...The Garde
Marina	OLIVE TOWNEND	Fifth Tableau	The Children of Bori
Hostess	EDITH CLEGG	**ACT III.**	
Varlaam	ROBERT RADFORD	Sixth Tableau... ...	...The Revolt
Missail ... ...·...	ALFRED HEATHER	Seventh Tableau ...	The Death of the Tsar
The Idiot	MAURICE D'OISLY		
Chelkalov	HERBERT LANGLEY		
Commissary	ALBERT CHAPMAN	CONDUCTORS FOR THE SEASON ...	Sir THOMAS BEECHAM
Two Jesuits	L. MORGAN and		Mr. PERCY PITT
	G. CLARKE		Mr. JULIUS HARRISON
			Mr. EUGENE GOOSSENS, Jr.
			Mr. HAROLD HOWELL
CONDUCTOR ...	Sir THOMAS BEECHAM.	Stage Director ...	Mr. GEORGE KING
		Assistant Stage Manager	Mr. JOSEPH KINSBERGEN
		Chorus Master ...	Mr HAROLD HOWELL

Seats may be booked at Forsyth Bros. Ltd., 126 Deansgate (Tel. 1100 Central) and at the Theatre Box Office (Tel. City 1787).

Walton's programme for *Boris Godounov*, 1916.

Sir Thomas Beecham, Lancashire's leading musician. He was the son of the inventor of Beecham's Powders. He was to influence Walton's life on key occasions, being involved with the commissioning of the Viola Concerto and *Belshazzar's Feast*.

In Oldham there were nearly as many pubs as there were mills – or so it must have seemed to Charles Walton on the eve of his son's scholarship audition; one drink led to another and with them went the cash for the journey to Oxford.

Choir schools cast their nets wide in search of the purest young voices: class and education were less important than musical talent.

CHORISTERSHIPS.

There will be a TRIAL OF VOICES on Thursday, June 27. Candidates must have a good Ear and a good Voice and should be between nine and twelve years of age. For particulars apply to the Precentor before June 22.

After what must have been a furious row, Mrs Walton decided there was nothing for it but to take Billie to Oxford herself. On tenterhooks, the boy waited outside while his mother borrowed the missing fare money from the local grocer.

"It was my first long train journey. I remember being very sick on the way."

Scene from *At the Haunted End of the Day* – Walton's film biography, directed by Tony Palmer.

CHAPTER 2

A SUPERIOR EDUCATION
1912–1920

"Oxford was the most beautiful place I had ever seen."

Christ Church Cathedral School, Oxford, by D. J. Godfrey.

FOR A BOY OF TEN who was the apple of his mother's eye and had never previously been south of Lancashire, the process of moving to a small boarding school in Oxford was inevitably something of a trauma. Not that the Cathedral Choir School was in any way Dickensian; less than two dozen boys resided there – six to a dormitory – in a pleasant, custom-built house across St Aldate's road from Christ Church, cared for and taught by a staff of eight. All the same, William remembered his first term as horrid: "the problem was I had a broad Lancashire accent and the other boys used to sit on my head until I spoke the same as they did – properly". But he soon settled in to a routine in which school work and music lessons (the boys were encouraged to try their hand at composition) were slotted in between daily choir practices and services, for which the boys dressed in three-piece suits with stiff Eton collars; they marched around the town in long gowns and square black hats that gave them the air of novice monks. Walton's weekly letters back home gave little away about whatever mischief the boys got up to but they provide a record of

steady achievement, goals scored at football, anthems sung in chapel, new-fangled aeroplanes seen in the sky. In due course the probationary status was removed; he became a full chorister and eventually head boy. The school's magazines give details of the prizes he won and the concerts in which he performed.

He was twelve when the Great War broke out. There was talk of his having to return to Oldham because his father, deprived of pupils and therefore of cash, could no longer keep up his contributions to his son's education. (Noel Walton, then fourteen, was taken out of school and sent to work as an office clerk.) The Dean of Christ Church, Thomas Strong, came to Billie's rescue, paying the balance of the fees not covered by Walton's choral scholarship. Dr Strong, later Bishop of Ripon and then Oxford, was a great encourager of the boy's talent, which was evinced as early as 1914 with the composition of *Variations for Violin and Piano on a chorale by J.S.B.* The work (apparently only a fragment) has not survived; Walton later wrote of it (and of his other early compositions) in his usual self-deprecating, staccato manner: "not very interesting and wisely decided to stop. However broke loose again about 13 [actually 14] and wrote two 4-part songs, 'Tell me where is fancy bred?' and 'Where the bee sucks'. After that fairly went in for it [composition] and produced about 30 very bad works of various species, songs, motets, Magnificats etc."

Walton was notoriously dismissive and unreliable about his work. He omits mention of both a *Choral Fantasia* for organ performed in the cathedral by Dr Ley and his *Litany*, the most striking of his early compositions, to a text by the seventeenth-century poet Phineas Fletcher, which begins "Drop, drop, slow tears". (It was originally composed for four equal treble voices; he later re-wrote it for a choir of mixed voices.) The organ piece is lost; the *Litany*'s manuscript is dated "Easter 1916", a few weeks after the disastrous battle of Verdun, an event which may have contributed to the music's prevailing emotion of tragic loss. When Walton was confirmed on March 15th (a fortnight before his fourteenth birthday and soon after Verdun) the Dean presented him with an inscribed bible. He left it behind, his brother thought on purpose, when he next went home to Oldham: organised religion held no attraction for him despite (or perhaps because of) his daily involvement at Christ Church.

As the war entered its third year, the streets of Oxford were filled with young servicemen, some preparing to go to the Western Front, others invalided out and recuperating in the many hospitals established in the Oxford colleges. The war made itself felt even within the closely-knit community of the school; Walton wrote home that they had been planting vegetables in the garden – he planted out his cress in the shape of a letter "W" – and urged his mother not to forget to apply for a ration card for his holiday visit. The boys were taken to see a documentary feature film *The Battle of the Somme*. Too young to fight, Walton's personal crisis was more mundane: his voice broke. Dr Strong was a keen amateur pianist and a lover of contemporary music; he was loath to lose a

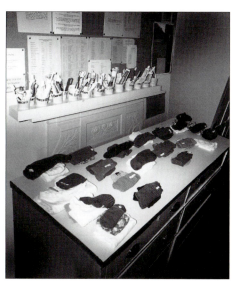

There were 21 pupils at the school. Each choirboy is still responsible for his own socks and dental hygiene.

young man whose talent was proving to be exceptional. "He does not think it right that we should let Billy go", the choir school's headmaster reported to Walton's father. Walton stayed on at the school, still singing solos but now in a bass register. He began to concentrate on composition. We can safely ignore Walton's frivolous claim that he took to writing music merely to make himself interesting and thus avoid this second threat of being sent back to Oldham. The eminent composer Sir Hubert Parry – visiting

Oxford as an examiner for the music degrees – looked through a bundle of the manuscripts that Walton had left for Dr Strong after one of the regular Sunday morning informal seminars he held for the senior boys and observed "There's a lot in this chap, you must keep your eye on him." Walton later met Parry and told his mother that he "had quite a long talk with him. He is an awfully jolly old person." (He died the following year.) Other distinguished Oxford academics, among them the next Professor of Music, Hugh Allen, were coaching him in different aspects of music. Dr Walker gave lectures on harmony; Dr Iliffe on part-writing. "He says I have done wonderfully well at my counterpoint and thinks I shall easily be able to get through my first Mus. Bac . . . I expect to be able to do florid counterpoint in four parts before half term." These were warm-hearted forward-looking teachers: Dr Strong played through Schœnberg's latest piano music (the *Six Little Pieces*) and Dr Allen introduced him to Stravinsky's *Petroushka*. Walton also spent many hours in the Ellis Library in the Radcliffe Camera reading orchestral scores by Debussy, Ravel and Stravinsky. He was only sixteen when he passed the first part of the Bachelor of Music examinations with flying colours.

Later that year, 1918, Walton was awarded a two-year in-college Exhibition worth £85 per annum at Christ Church, thus becoming, at the Dean's instigation, one of the youngest undergraduates ever to enter the university. "In a way it is rather a plunge from a small school into the University" Dr Strong told him; "some boys might make a great mess of things, but I think this will not be the case with you." He was assigned a room in Peckwater

Quadrangle, equipped with a handsome Bechstein upright piano, and over the next two years he progressed both socially and creatively at a prodigious rate. He was well-liked in the college, serving as cox of the second college boat for the bumping races. He also enjoyed a modest career as a performer: in his first term he stood in for a month as the chapel organist at Brasenose College, earning £2 a service. In the month the Great War ended he went to three performances given in Oxford by the Carl Rosa Opera, *Madam Butterfly, Faust* and *Mignon.* "They were done very well for a travelling company", he wrote to his mother, a confident assessment for somebody who at the time had never attended an opera performance in London. In the creative field the short songs and choral compositions of his early teens were superseded by a four-movement Piano Quartet, his first substantial work; it runs for close on half an hour and was probably suggested as a composing task by the new professor, Hugh Allen. (It was later selected for publication by the Carnegie Trust, for whom Allen and Vaughan Williams were adjudicators.) The Piano Quartet was the first of Walton's compositions to reveal a mind grappling with the concept of musical development. There are echoes in it of Elgar and Frank Bridge as well as the new European masters Ravel and Stravinsky, but the authentic Waltonian voice is already audible, in the romantic sweep of the quartet's melodies, the pungency of its rhythms and the recurring evidence of a musical mind struggling with formal problems. While it is erroneous to suggest, as commentators tend to do, that Walton was entirely self-taught, the quartet confirms that his was a natural talent of the first order. As he sipped sherry at Dean Strong's and pored over new music at the Ellis Library he had been assimilating musical ideas at a great rate.

His contemporaries as well as his elders were quick to recognise his gifts. The poet Roy Campbell, then seventeen and another outsider, newly arrived in Oxford from South Africa, described him as a real genius, "one of the finest fellows I ever met . . . It was soon apparent that we were not cut out for scholars of the routine sort. William was already equipped for greatness, with a metaphorical self-starter and internal combustion." Campbell noted ecstatically that his new friend demonstrated "a sort of inward exhilaration, as if lifted by invisible wings. His accent varied according to his mood, and sudden animation or excitement was sure to reveal the traces of a broad Lancashire accent underlying the more polished accent he had acquired at Oxford."

In his second college term, early in 1919, Walton befriended a Canadian poet, Frank Prewett, also studying at Christ Church, through whom he met the poets John Masefield and Siegfried Sassoon. "They are great men" he wrote to his mother. Sassoon had a private fortune and was to become one of Walton's most generous supporters. But the most significant encounter was with Sacheverell Sitwell, then 21, who was depressed by the lack of "buzz" in the university (the war had only just ended) and exclaimed to his older brother Osbert, 26, that Walton was "the sole redeeming point of Oxford". A memorable tea party ensued when Sassoon took the Sitwell brothers to visit Walton, still only sixteen, in his blue wall-papered room. The dining table was decorated, Osbert noted in *Laughter in the Next Room*, with an enormous plate of bananas, thus creating "an almost ostentatious sense of luxury". Sitwell's description of the encounter only hints at the colossal charm the sixteen-year-old boy exercised on all who met him. He had the pale colouring, Sitwell wrote, of a young Scandinavian with "a rather tall, slight figure . . . [and a] long, narrow, delicately shaped head". He singled out Walton's bird-like profile and the high dome of his brow, the sure mark of an intellectual. "Sensitiveness rather than toughness was the quality at first most apparent in him. He appeared to be excessively shy . . .

Music showed a way out of the constraint and after tea we pressed him to play some of his compositions for us. Accordingly he got up from the table and then sat down at the piano, the few steps between clearly indicating the burden of his hospitality, a feeling of strain, almost of hopelessness, combined with that of a need for intense concentration." He played them the slow movement of his new piano quartet and according to Osbert botched it so badly that it was difficult to judge the merits of the work. But he was obviously a *wunderkind* and the Sitwells adopted him forthwith. The cosmopolitanism of his new friends is reflected in his subsequent letters home: on June 17, 1919 he wrote: "I am going to London on Wednesday to stay with the Sitwells. Our concert [music by an older protégé of the Sitwells, Bernard van Dieren] never came off . . . however as a consolation some of my songs are going to be sung at Lady Glenconner's concert in London on Friday. Also I shall be conducting two pieces for orchestra at the Russian Ballet."

In November he heard Alfred Cortot give a recital in Oxford. "He is simply magnificent . . . Lady Ottoline Morrell asked me over to her house [at Garsington] last Sunday. It was very entertaining. I went to London yesterday for the afternoon and saw the new ballet *Parade*." Still only a teenager, the world seemed at his feet. There remained the thorny questions of his formal education and his upkeep. Three times in 1919 he failed Responsions, the examinations without which he could never take a degree. Christ Church had no alternative but to suspend his place, but very decently they gave him £150 with which to settle his "liabilities". To tide him over, the Sitwell brothers invited him to stay with them in London. "I went for a few weeks", Walton said, "and stayed about fifteen years."

Although officially rusticated, the university was still prepared to allow him to sit his Mus. Bac. He passed the second stage in June 1920 and returned for a time to live in college, but without his Responsions there was no way he could remain an undergraduate and down he went. So the Sitwells had triumphed over the equally generous but less exotic appeal of the Oxford establishment represented by Dr Strong and Sir Hugh Allen. Walton claimed that the academics wanted him to study at one of the London music colleges and then become a schoolmaster: "That was my career as mapped out by them, and I saw that coming and withdrew." But the evidence suggests that from his Oxford schooldays Walton was determined to follow the life of a composer; he never had any intention of submitting to a long academic apprenticeship. Roy Campbell was in awe of what he described as young Walton's "sense of vocation and how a man can live for his art".

Let us prune the tree of language
Of its dead fruit.
Let us melt up all the clichés
Into molten metal;
Fashion weapons that will scold and flay;
Let us curb this eternal Humour
And become witty.

A stanza from
"How Shall We Rise To Greet The Dawn?", published
1919, in *Argonaut and Juggernaut* by Osbert Sitwell.

The Headmaster, the Rev. Edward Peake, staff and pupils of Christ Church Choir School, 1912. Walton is in the front row, extreme right (enlarged below).

— 1912 —

CATHEDRAL CHOIR HOUSE, OXFORD.

Dear Mother we have had a very nice time the fortnight. We had a lovely prize giving, the boys being dressed up. One Saturday we went to the Deans to tea and he showed us the State in which Charles I slept in. We went up the watch tower as well. We won our first match by three goals to none yesterday against Malbrough House. I did

OXFORD 8.30 p.m. 17 NOV 12

Walton
Werneth Hall Rd
Oldham
Lancs.

Walton wrote home to mother every week.

Choristers still walk back and forth from School to Chapel twice a day.

24

The Concert

79

PROGRAMME.

PART I.

1. Songs of Innocence, Op. 4			Walford Davies.
	(a) "The Lamb."		
	(b) "A cradle song."		
	(c) "Infant joy."		
	(d) "The Shepherd."		
2. Piano Duet	Hungarian Dances, No. 5		Brahms.
	C. H. L. Bartrum and D. C. G. Dickinson.		
3. Part Song	"To Daffodils."		Basil Harwood.
4. Recitation	"The Three Questions."		Anon.
	H. Foster Martin.		
5. Piano Solo	"Studies."		Bach.
	G. W. Proger.		
6. Part Songs—			
	(a) "Greeting"		} Mendelssohn.
	(b) "The Passage-bird's farewell."		
	(c) "O wert thou in the cauld Blast."		
7. Recitation	"A Wonderful Cure."		Anon.
	N. C. Wright.		

PART II.

1. Part Song	"Coronach."		Schubert.
2. Piano Solo	"Morning Song."		Dnnhill.
	S. H. Staff.		
3. Violin Solo—			
	(a) "Spring."		Dr. Arne.
	(b) "Hey Baloo."		Schumann.
	W. T. Walton.		
4. Part Song	"Ave Maria."		Brahms.
5. Piano Duet	"La Nursery" (Nos. 2 and 9)		Ingelbrecht.
	J. A. Chubb and S. L. L. Russell.		
6. Part Songs—			
	(a) "Autumn Song."		} Mendelssohn.
	(b) "The Harvest Field."		
7. Duologue	"Chestnuts."		
	L. H. Macklin and A. B. G. Dickinson.		

School Christmas Concert, 1912. Walton played two violin solos. "Our exile from home at Christmas" (wrote the school magazine) "was enlivened in the usual way . . . we might have been Bulgarians from the way we attacked the turkey."

Prominent Oxford musicians, all organists. From left to right: Sir Hugh Allen, Varley Roberts and Henry Ley. Ley was organist of Christ Church. He encouraged Walton's early compositions for the organ. "This morning Mr Ley played my Choral Fantasia after service. People said it was very fine, but I don't give my opinion."

The Dean, the Rev. Thomas B. Strong, later Bishop of Ripon and then Oxford. "In those days the senior boys used to come to my house every Sunday morning after Cathedral – i.e. about 11.30 a.m.", Dr Strong recalled. "It began by being a sort of little Bible class; but they gradually developed the habit of staying till 1 p.m. and messing about with my books, etc. I think, but am not quite sure that W. used to strum on my piano."

A Litany, Walton's first preserved composition. March 1916.

THE KING'S VISIT TO OXFORD.

King George V visited Oxford in 1916. Walton stood "about 3 yards away from him".

Oxford was the headquarters of the Royal Flying Corps during the First World War. The RFC used Tom Quad, Christ Church, as a parade ground.

Wounded officers convalescing in Oxford were a familiar sight to young Walton.

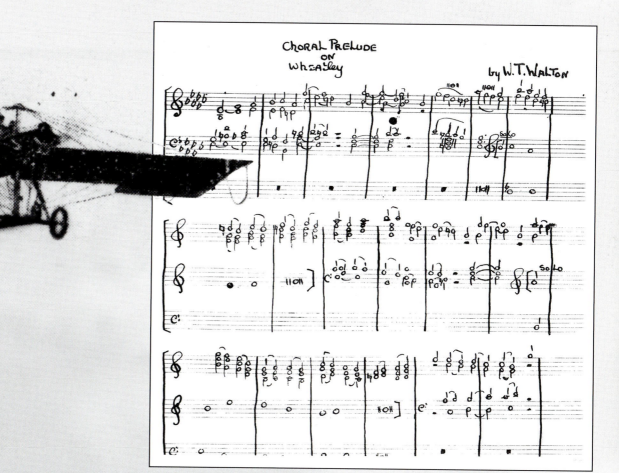

Walton's Choral Prelude *Wheatley*.

Christ Church
Oxford

Dear Mother,

Thanks very much for the parcel and 1/-. H. G. Ley came back on Thursday. I showed my six part Motet. He said it had wonderful ideas in it. I showed him the others. They were quite excellent especially the Fantasia which I hadn't finished copying out. A new Choral Prelude and two others didn't sound well on the organ but were fairly respectable on the piano. He is teaching me harmony free and is going over the the motets, and I thing we may sing them Bath. Macklin and Winnifrith have not yet come back. We went to Wheatley on Wednesday. Some areoplanes have been over. One looped the loop. Ð D.r Sandy preached this morning. By the way, he is seeing us to the Battle of the Somme. There is no more news.

With much love

Billy

Walton's letter
to mother
10 September
1916.

Walton won the
school composition
prize when he was
only fourteen.

Prize-Giving, Friday, Nov. 3rd, 1916, at 3.45 p.m.

OXFORD LOCAL EXAMINATIONS.

JUNIOR (*given by the Dean and Chapter*).
2nd Class Honours—L. H. MACKLIN.
3rd Class Honours—F. D. HAM.
    G. SHAW.
    C. G. WINDLE.
Pass—W. T. WALTON.
    J. P. H. JACOBS.

JUNIOR (*given by the Headmaster*).
Pass— S. H. STAFF.
    D. R. AXTELL.

PRELIMINARY (*given by Dr. Watson*).
    G. W. RAKE.
    A. C. E. DEVEREUX.
    W. E. COLEMAN.
    J. E. FRANCIS.
    C. B. WINNIFRITH.

PRELIMINARY (*given by the Headmaster*).
    S. C. BOWLEY.

CERTIFICATES (*second time*).
    V. A. H. CLEMENTS.
    A. J. C. B. GILL.

THE DEAN'S PRIZE (Distinction in Latin)
    —L. H. MACKLIN.

HISTORY PRIZE (*given by F. H. Wright, Esq.*), (Distinction in History)—W. T. WALTON.

PROGRESS (*given by the Headmaster*)—R. B. NEWMAN.

CHOIR WORK (*given by Mr. Ley*)—L. H. MACKLIN.

MUSIC—Senior (*given by Mr. and Mrs. Allchin*):W. T. WALTON. Junior (*given by Miss Allchin*): J. E. FRANCIS.

CERTIFICATES OF THE ASSOCIATED
BOARD R.A.M. AND R.C.M.
Lower— L. H. MACKLIN, F. D. HAM, D. R. AXTELL, C. B. WINNIFRITH.
Elementary—V. A. H. CLEMENTS, A. J. C. B. GILL, J. P. H. JACOBS.
Primary— W. E. COLEMAN, A. C. E. DEVEREUX, J. E. FRANCIS, G. W. RAKE.

SCHOOL HONOURS.
Military Cross—
    G. W. THACKER (left 1908).
    W. G. T. EDWARDS (left 1911).

WHEN YOU'RE A LONG, LONG WAY FROM HOME (2).

When you're a long, long way from home, it makes you feel like you're alone,
It's hard to find a pal that's true, that you can tell your troubles to,
And when you send a letter home, your mother's voice rings in your ears,
And then you cross the t's with kisses, what a strange world this is!
Then you dot the i's with tears, and all the sunshine turns to gloom
When you're a long, long way from home.

BY ARRANGEMENT WITH MESSRS. FRANCIS, DAY & HUNTER, THE PUBLISHERS OF THE MUSIC.

BAMFORTH COPYRIGHT.

Had he been a few years older, Walton would have been among the million "Tommies" writing home to mother from the Western Front.

CHRIST CHURCH, OXFORD.

Oct 8th 1916

Dear Mother,
The weather has been awful this last week. We have had hardly any games. I haven't had a letter this week.

Walton's letter to mother, 8 October 1916.

The Dean has been saying somethink to me about the Royal College of Music .. He says "it is unpatriotic to England to let slip such a Musical brain.

8 October 1916

CHRIST CHURCH, OXFORD.

Sept 30th 1917

Dear Mother
I won the Senior Cup. And also the 100 yds & mile & ½ mile. And in the jumps both the High & the Long.. For the 100 yds I got a cup for that, a gamedish & for the ½ mile a silver tray. & for the High Jump I got salt & pepper shakers. In the Long jump prize I changed my watch for a 7/6 Ingersoll which could be made into a clock or you can carry it in your pocket. It is fine. I went to Dr Allens on Thursday. We began football on Friday. I went to Dr Allens yesterday He played me most of Otello. I went to early service this morning. Dr Ottley preached! The anthem tonight is "where thou reignest" Schubert. There is no more news

With much love
Billy

30 September 1917

We went to bed at 9.0 & about 9.30 suddenly the lights went out downstairs and the hooter began going. Then Mr Peake came up to us, and the other dormitory which is on the top landing, and told us to go down stairs since there was a raid. Having arrived down in the drawing room (there were 10 of us) we sat ourselves round the fire, and had candles for lights. Then the "specials" came round and said all lights out and we were left in the dark. We stayed down till 11.30 but heard nothing.

21 October 1917

Half-term begins on Thursday. Prize-giving on Friday. I have two prizes, the Deans and Choir. Send me some chink to go to the Opera with.
With much love
Billy.

4 November 1917

We did not go to the Deans as he is away. I had a solo in the anthem to-night. 96 is "Dies Irae", Mozart.

December 1917 (exact date not given).

We are all working hard in the garden sowing vegetables and things. By the way you must get my ration card for the holidays. Don't forget.
My exam is on 19th. I hope to just manage to scrape through, but it will be a near thing.

3 March 1918

A scene from the feature length documentary: *The Battle of the Somme*. Walton and his fellow choristers attended a showing at the Electric Cinema in Oxford in November 1916; the film's harrowing scenes would have brought home the reality of trench warfare.

Sir Hubert Parry (1848–1918), the composer of *Jerusalem*, spotted Walton's talent early on.

Dear Mother

I hope you are getting on well. The weather has been stormy and a little colder than last week. I went to see Sir Hubert Parry on last Sunday afternoon and had quite a long talk with him. He is an awfully jolly old person. We had a game on Monday. I had a lesson at 10.30. I went to see Dr Allen on Tuesday afternoon. He has asked Macklin and I to go to a rehearsal of the Bach choir Orchestra at 8.30.

Walton's letter to mother, 24 June 1917.

Christ Church Cathedral.

Walton's 1917 school report. He was fifteen. "Tomorrow the exams begin. I shall try very hard to pass. Don't forget to send me the money, by return of post, if not already being sent. There is no more news."

CHRIST CHURCH CATHEDRAL SCHOOL,
OXFORD.

WEEKLY REPORT.

Name Walton   Date Nov. 4   1917

Form.	No. of Boys in Form.	Place last week.	Place this week.
Senior work.			

Remarks   very fair.

E. P.

Walton's early *Valse* for piano solo dated 2 February 1917.

The Radcliffe Camera, one of Oxford's most intriguing buildings. It houses the Ellis Library, which contained a good selection of scores by leading contemporary European composers. "I fear I spent too much time there, to the detriment of my scholarly studies in Latin, Greek and Algebra."

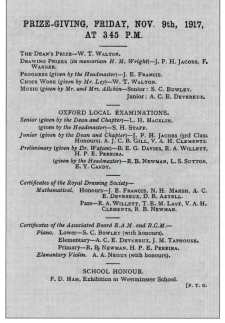

PRIZE-GIVING, FRIDAY, NOV. 9th, 1917,
AT 3.45 P.M.

THE DEAN'S PRIZE—W. T. WALTON.
DRAWING PRIZES (*in memoriam H. M. Wright*)—J. P. H. JACOBS, F. WARNER.
PROGRESS (*given by the Headmaster*)—J. E. FRANCIS.
CHOIR WORK (*given by Mr. Ley*)—W. T. WALTON.
MUSIC (*given by Mr. and Mrs. Allchin*—Senior: S. C. BOWLEY.
Junior: A. C. E. DEVEREUX.

OXFORD LOCAL EXAMINATIONS.
Senior (*given by the Dean and Chapter*)—L. H. MACKLIN.
(*given by the Headmaster*)—S. H. STAFF.
Junior (*given by the Dean and Chapter*)—J. P. H. JACOBS (3rd Class Honours). A. J. C. B. GILL, V. A. H. CLEMENTS.
Preliminary (*given by Dr. Watson*)—B. E. G. DAVIES, R. A. WILLETT, H. P. E. PEREIRA.
(*given by the Headmaster*)—R. B. NEWMAN, L. S. SUTTON, E. Y. CANDY.

Certificates of the Royal Drawing Society—
Mathematical. Honours—J. E. FRANCIS, N. H. MARSH, A. C. E. DEVEREUX, D. R. AXTELL.
Pass—R. A. WILLETT, T. E. M. LAST, V. A. H. CLEMENTS, R. B. NEWMAN.

Certificates of the Associated Board R.A.M. and R.C.M.—
Piano. Lower—S. C. BOWLEY (with honours).
Elementary—A. C. E. DEVEREUX, J. M. TAPHOUSE.
Primary—R. B. NEWMAN, H. P. E. PEREIRA.
Elementary Violin. A. A. NEGUS (with honours).

SCHOOL HONOUR.
F. D. HAM, Exhibition at Westminster School.
[P. T. O.

At the annual prize-giving in November 1917, Walton won a prize from the Dean and another for his work in the choir. He continued to sing solos even after his voice broke.

The Dean's prize is awarded to Walton. He is head boy and is helpful to me in that position and shows great promise in music. He has been encouraged in musical composition so far that he attends the lectures of Dr Walker and Dr Allen. When a little while ago we were disturbed by a Zeppelin alarm, he at once proceeded to sit down with his music manuscript. I suppose if there had been a bomb "thus" dropped, there would have been some discordant crashes in the bass! Walton also receives Mr Ley's prize for work in the Choir.

Extract from Headmaster Peake's journal, 1917.

31

Walton's letter to mother, 16 July 1918.

Dr Strong wanted Walton to study at the University; "He is now out of the choir and cannot go on indefinitely in the school. I am anxious that he should have the best chance he can get of doing well in music."

Like Belshazzar's before him, Walton's fate hung in the balance.

In 1931 his oratorio on Belshazzar and the Jewish exiles scored a huge triumph.

Rembrandt's painting was later reproduced in the published score.

Tom Quad, Christ Church, Oxford. Walton, aged sixteen, became an undergraduate of the College in October 1918, a few weeks before the end of the Great War.

Dear Mother

Thanks for your letter and the £1. I have been and am and shall be very busy. The Dean has made all arrangements about sheets etc. And I can go to him for money when I am without.

I have a most lovely Bechstein upright in my rooms. I am taking both organ and piano lessons from Mr Ley now as Mr Allchin is too busy with the military.

The 'flu' is getting quite the rage round here. I don't know what it is like at home. Mr Marshall one of the choirmen got it and died last night.

I went to the Musical Club last night.

It was a fine performance. The Catterall quartett is coming soon. We are having a memorial service to Parry. Everything goes very smoothly. We haven't had any fun worth speaking of. Except our Musical quartett make a 'hell' of a din.

I have been out to tea with Roy and he has been round to me. I have also been out to Mr Reakes and Mr Ley to tea. There is nothing else to say.

With much love

Billy

Walton's letter to mother, 23 October 1918.

Roy Campbell, the South African poet, a year older than Walton, was one of his first undergraduate friends. "We went to the same tutor of Greek," Campbell wrote in his memoirs, "and we became very good friends. We walked out with two young ladies who were also very good friends, and who were employed as waitresses. Needless to say, Willie's one eventually became a Countess. Something magical seems to happen to every thing he touches . . ."

Christ Church 2nd Eight, 1919.

Frank Prewett, a Canadian poet, was another keen oarsman. He introduced Walton to the poet Siegfried Sassoon.

Walton (bottom centre) was cox of the college's 2nd boat. He weighed only 8st. 9lbs. At the Choir School he had been very athletic, winning the long jump, the high jump, the quarter mile and the half mile as well as playing football (inside right and goalie) and cricket (he once scored 45 runs).

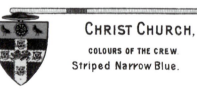

CHRIST CHURCH,

COLOURS OF THE CREW.

Striped Narrow Blue.

I have started rowing. It is great sport. Next term I shall cox the 'House' eight. I don't know whether there will be any races. Well, I can't think of anything else to say.

With much love

Billy

Walton coxing with his College Eight, 1919. He consolidated his success as cox the previous year: "We've had races for the last two days. We beat Campion Hall in the heats, St John's in the semi-final and Balliol in the final. So we are the victors."

Walton's letter to mother,
6 November 1918.

35

Siegfried Sassoon (1887–1967) painted by Glyn Philpot in 1919. Controversial war poet and hero, he was fifteen years older than Walton. He introduced the young composer to Lady Ottoline Morrell, who held court at Garsington Manor outside Oxford.

THE D'OYLY CARTE OPERA COMPANY.

REPERTOIRE.

Wednesday, Matinee, and Thursday, Evening, "THE MIKADO."

Wednesday, Evening, and Saturday, Evening, "YEOMEN OF THE GUARD."

Friday, "TRIAL BY JURY" and "PIRATES OF PENZANCE."

Saturday, Matinee, "THE GONDOLIERS."

Playbill for the D'Oyly Carte company's Oxford performances in November 1919. Walton saw *The Mikado*.

Umbrellas by Dorothy Brett. Lady Ottoline Morrell (centre) is pictured with her friends: Lytton Strachey, Aldous Huxley, Dorothy Brett, Julian Morrell, Katherine Mansfield, John Middleton Murry and Mark Gertler. Lady Ottoline (1873–1938) was a leading patroness of the English literary and artistic world. Her bohemian house parties were crowded with famous personalities, among them D.H. Lawrence and Augustus John.

Walton in 1919 aged seventeen.

"Zverov and Lopokova limbering up backstage before a performance of *Parade*, London 1919" by Dame Laura Knight.
"It was very marvellous", Walton told his mother, "especially the scenery [by Picasso]. The music was by Erik Satie, a Frenchman."

"The Sitwells were a rum lot"

declared Walton. "The father was an eccentric baronet called 'Ginger'. Their mother had been in prison for debt."

Osbert Sitwell (1892–1969) was a leading figure in London literary life. His first book of poems appeared in 1919 and his friendships extended to an older generation of wealthy art patrons. He was an intellectual entrepreneur who knew everybody worth knowing, including the poets T.S. Eliot and Ezra Pound.

Sacheverell Sitwell (1897–1988), the youngest of the three literary Sitwells. It was from "Sachie" that Walton acquired his love of books, painting and architecture. Sacheverell's initial opinion of Walton: "He certainly gave the impression of not having had very much to eat."

Edith Sitwell (1887–1964), the eldest of the three Sitwells. Her looks were as striking as her verse. She lived in a dingy flat in Bayswater and entertained her admiring circle with weak tea and penny buns. Her companion and former governess, Helen Rootham, was one of the first to sing Walton's early songs *The Winds*.

Members of the Sitwell circle sketched at "The Golden Cross" by artist Gabriel Atkin – clockwise from the head of the table: Osbert Sitwell, Wilfred Childe, Gerald Crowe, Frank Prewett, Sacheverell Sitwell, Atkin, V. da Sola Pinto, Siegfried Sassoon and Thomas Earp.

Walton's letter to mother, 29 June 1919.

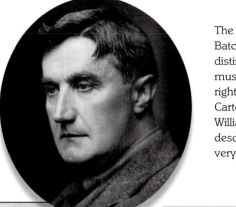

The examiners for the 1920 Batchelor of Music degree were distinguished members of the musical establishment. Left to right: Sir Hugh Allen, Percy Carter Buck and Ralph Vaughan Williams, who Walton later described as "a pussy cat with very sharp claws".

Trinity Term. 1920

Names of candidates who, on June 8th 1920, having been examined in accordance with the Statutes for the ~~their~~ Second Examination for the Degree of Bachelor of Music, have satisfied us the examiners

Berkeyfield   George.   Queen's College
Boulton   Cecil Dudley Clair.   Exeter
Leonard   Stuart Berrington   Merton
Marriott   Horace DD.   Keble
Spence   Horace   Corpus Christi
Walton   William Turner   Christ Church

                    H. P. Allen Prof. Mus.
                    Percy C. Buck.
                    Ralph Vaughan Williams.

"If you are going to adopt music as your service you must be sure you realise what her service demands. You will find her a loveable but stern mistress who demands all your good will – all your energy, all your wits and all your time. The musical training that you must go through before you are admitted of her house is by no means light. You may fiddle outside the door for hours at a time & never see her face. You may tire yourself out on a keyboard . . . with every sign of prowess & yet not get the door opened. No short cut can manage an entry. No wireless message or telephone calls are of any use. You are admitted to her freedom only by serving a full & thorough apprenticeship which means you have learned thoroughly all those things upon which music rests & without which no performance, no teaching, no composition is well grounded and therefore safe."

From lecture notes by Sir Hugh Allen, Professor of Music, Oxford University.

Walton passed the second part of his B.Mus. degree in June 1920.

39

"I never could pass those damned exams …"

Walton, William Turner

PRELIMINARY EXAMINATION passed *Hilary Term 1918*

Name sent in from *Christ Church*

MATRICULATED *May 20th 1918* at *Christ Church*

DEGREE OF BACHELOR OF MUSIC.

FIRST EXAMINATION for the Degree of B. MUS. passed . } *June 11th 1918.*

SECOND EXAMINATION for the Degree of B. MUS. passed . } *June 8th 1920.*

THIRD EXAMINATION for the Degree of B. MUS. passed . }

EXERCISE :—

Received from Candidate by the Secretary to the Boards of Faculties . }

Deposited by the Secretary in the Bodleian Library }

Date of ADMISSION to the Degree of BACHELOR OF MUSIC

Walton failed to complete the Third Examination in his Bachelor of Music degree. His inability to master the rudiments of Greek, Latin and Algebra was his undoing.

CHAPTER 3

THE ARTFUL LODGER

1920–1929

"Not only were the girls frequent, but numerous"

OSBERT SITWELL ON WALTON

Pulcinella and Arlecchino, Walton's favourite commedia dell'arte figures. Frontispiece to the published collection of Edith Sitwell's *Façade* poems. The artist was Gino Severini (1883–1966), the Italian futurist painter who was a friend of the Sitwells and decorated the walls of Castel Montegufoni with murals.

L ESS THAN A DECADE HAD GONE BY since Billie's farewell to the smoky chimneys of Oldham and its gaunt, malevolent mills. At Oxford the daily grind of choir practice and Sung Eucharist had given way to the creative and social excitements of university life and now, thanks to the generosity of the Sitwell brothers, under whose roof he lived throughout the dazzling twenties, the dreaming spires were to be replaced on his horizon by the elegant squares, artists' studios and bohemian pubs of Chelsea. Dr Strong must have approved: in the spring of 1921 he gave Walton a further £50 for a visit to Italy and Sicily with the Sitwells. The young man fell under the spell of the Mediterranean as soon as the night train emerged from the tunnels that skirt the Ligurian Sea and he glimpsed the morning sun glinting on the water.

The Sitwells offered Walton both style and substance. They were the self-consciously aesthetic children of Sir George Sitwell, an eccentric baronet who had homes at Renishaw Hall in Derbyshire and Castel Montegufoni in Tuscany. The sibling trio combined good taste and intellectual curiosity with a predilection for hard, productive work. Edith, tall, attenuated and elegant, was the oldest, not quite 35 when "Willie" appeared on the scene and already making a name for herself as an experimental poet and editor. Osbert, Roman patrician in looks, was a witty spokesman for everything progressive; he and his younger brother Sacheverell, poet and belles-lettrist, shared a house and a common cause: to shake up the bourgeoisie. As Aldous Huxley put it, "their great object is to REBEL". (Huxley especially admired "their toreador attitude to the bloody-bloodies of the world".)

Walton was the Sitwells' "adopted or elected brother". With his long nose and beautiful hands he even resembled Edith in looks. The trio were genuinely happy to support gifted young artists but (to be harsh for a moment) the presence about the house of an undisputed young genius such as Walton at dinner parties and cultural soirées also enhanced their artistic standing. Osbert in particular had a gift for self-promotion to rival that of Jean Cocteau in France. There's no dispute concerning the Sitwells' importance to Walton: they introduced him to everybody who was anybody in the international artistic world. Osbert summed up their contribution accurately (if a shade immodestly) in his memoir, *Laughter in the Next Room:* "we were able to keep him in touch with the vital works of the age, with the music, for example, of Stravinsky, and to obtain for him, through the kindness of our old family friend [Professor] E.J. Dent, an introduction to Busoni, a modern master of counterpoint [not a fruitful meeting, as it happens; Ferrucio Busoni told his wife that Walton wrote "without imagination or feeling"] . . . He also had the benefit of consulting Ernest Ansermet on various problems of composition [more likely, conducting]. Moreover by travelling in our company in Italy, Spain and Germany, he soon acquired a knowledge of the arts, both past and present, belonging to those countries. It was noticeable from the first that he manifested an innate feeling for the masterpieces of painting and architecture, no less than of music: and inevitably the people, landscapes, festas and customs he observed increased the store of experience on which he could draw for the enriching of his work."

A self-confessed sponger in the pursuit of his art, Walton settled down happily in his cosy Chelsea "garret". He never gave lessons and politely refused an offer of work as a proof-reader (for a music publisher) organised for him by the well-meaning young conductor Adrian Boult. The writing of music, nothing else, was to be Walton's life and the winter of 1921–22, a few months before his twentieth birthday, saw the birth of his most astounding composition. *Façade* is a setting of alternately witty, child-like and nostalgic poems by Edith Sitwell for speaker and six interweaving, often jazz-inflected instruments. It was written in close collaboration with the Sitwell brothers and first presented with them acting as impresarios-cum-ringmasters in the drawing-room of their home at 2 Carlyle Square in Chelsea. Like most of Walton's major works, *Façade* was subject to many revisions, deletions and additions over the next thirty years before achieving its definitive form of twenty-one numbers. Two orchestral suites and a witty ballet by Frederick Ashton have added immeasurably to its popularity.

Another composition, of purely abstract music, was already in progress: a String Quartet commenced while still at Oxford and performed in 1921 in a two-movement form. Withdrawn while Walton composed a central Scherzo movement, it was subsequently selected by Osbert Sitwell's friend Professor Dent to be Britain's official entry at the first International Society of Contemporary Music Festival, held in Salzburg in 1923. The revision was completed in Amalfi, where Walton stayed with the Sitwells at a spectacular hillside hotel, formerly a Capuchin monastery. The quartet met with a mixed reception: the musicians who first performed it in London joked that it might sound better played backwards. The ladies' quartet from Liverpool who played in Salzburg "put up an abominable performance" according to Osbert Sitwell but the *Times* review praised their pluck and instead panned the music. The 21-year-old Walton was nevertheless treated as the leader of the British avant-garde and taken by Alban Berg to meet Arnold Schoenberg, an experience from which, happily, he emerged with only slight traces of atonalism.

If Walton's bright start seemed in danger of fizzling out at this period it was because he was subjecting himself to rigorous self-examination and fastidious selection of his material. The writer Cecil Gray praised "the slow, sure, steady way in which he has built himself up into a mature, self-reliant personality out of such comparatively unpromising beginnings, and in his art has acquired a formidable technical capacity which was lacking in his early days, by dint of sheer unremitting hard work." Walton wrote later about this period that he "produced some bad works in various styles, now mercifully in the fire". Among them was his first symphonic composition, an overture entitled *Dr Syntax*; it was inspired by a set of Rowlandson drawings, presumably introduced to him by the Sitwells, of the legendary Romney Marsh highwayman. Also "missing believed destroyed" are the arrangements of foxtrots he worked on in the early 1920s for a famous London hotel dance band, the Savoy Orpheans. Their leading spirit was the band-leader and arranger, Debroy Somers, a friend of a friend of the Sitwells. He appears to have prompted Walton to compose a substantial *Fantasia Concertante for* two pianos, jazz band and orchestra. The marriage of jazz and classical music was in the air: George Gershwin's *Rhapsody in Blue,* described as "an experiment in modern music", had just appeared. Walton met Gershwin and was fascinated by his music but confessed many years later that he "suddenly abandoned the jazz style in a fit of disgust", so the *Fantasia Concertante* manuscript, "monumentally planned" according to his friend Constant Lambert, went into the fire.

Another 1925 score by Walton that has vanished was the incidental music to a play by the Bloomsbury intellectual Lytton Strachey. *A Son of Heaven* was a tragic melodrama based on the 1900 Boxer Rising in China. Despite the oriental setting Walton could not resist including what Constant Lambert described as "some unmistakable traces of Gershwin . . . such was his obsession with ragtime".

While he was casting about for a truly personal style Walton helped out Lord Berners (a rich and eccentric member of the Sitwell circle) by orchestrating most of the numbers in *The Triumph of Neptune,* a ballet Berners composed for Diaghilev to a story line contributed by Sacheverell Sitwell. Walton had already performed a similar service for Constant Lambert, orchestrating at great speed Lambert's score for the ballet *Romeo and Juliet,* first heard in Monte Carlo in 1926. A witty all-rounder, Lambert was Walton's closest friend in the 1920s. He was only 21 when he charmed Diaghilev into granting him the ballet commission but Walton was turned down: the nearest he came to working for the Russian Ballet was to conduct his new orchestral overture, *Portsmouth Point,* as an entr'acte during Diaghilev's 1926 summer season at Her Majesty's Theatre. The breezy score radiates confidence: tuneful, cocky and every bit as rumbustious as the Rowlandson engraving from which it derives, it made an impressive orchestral début for Walton and was soon in demand from conductors looking for something fresh and tangy as an opening number for their concert programmes.

Hubert Foss's music department at Oxford University Press,

Line drawing of Edith Sitwell by Powys Evans.

with whom in 1926 Walton entered into what was to prove a life-time relationship, had a success on its hands. And the friendly rivalry which existed between himself and Lambert helped Walton to turn the creative corner. After conducting the première of a new work for chamber orchestra, *Siesta,* he took up the ballet score that Diaghilev had rejected and developed it as a piano concerto in all but name, the *Sinfonia Concertante.* The première was given under the auspices of the Royal Philharmonic Society with York Bowen as soloist and Ernest Ansermet conducting: the three movements were dedicated respectively to Osbert, Edith and Sachie Sitwell. It was another high point in his friendship with that extraordinarily influential family. Later that year, 1928, they were all to attend the successful Italian première of *Façade* in Siena (at another ISCM festival) and in 1929 Osbert began work on the text for the BBC commission that eventually became the oratorio *Belshazzar's Feast.*

At this time Walton was supported financially by Siegfried Sassoon, the love of whose life, Stephen Tennant, was also a good friend. Sassoon paid for Walton to accompany the tubercular Tennant, a scintillating personality of coruscating wit, on a winter holiday in the Bavarian Highlands. Acting as a nanny was hardly Walton's *métier* but he did it as a favour to his benefactor, who also paid for him to travel to Berlin to hear his music played. Cecil Beaton's elegant photographs of Walton cavorting with Tennant's high-camp circle of friends in fancy dress convey a measure of aristocratic languor on Walton's part yet he also kept company with waitresses (as Roy Campbell testified) and enjoyed boozy pub crawls with his male friends. Walton was on his way to becoming the great white hope of British music but emotionally he was still something of a dark horse. Living and travelling with the Sitwell brothers seems to have inhibited him: in his memoirs Osbert reported that Walton had many casual encounters with girls, but he generally fought shy of emotional relationships in his twenties. He was well-known in society circles and frequently mentioned by gossip columnists, but his name was never publicly linked with any particular woman until he met the German princess who was to be his first true love: Imma von Doernberg.

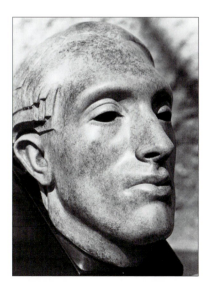

Bust of William Walton, 1925, by
Constant Lambert's brother Maurice.

"William had always to be near a piano." OSBERT SITWELL

E.J. Dent.

Ernest Ansermet.

Ferruccio Busoni.

Eugène Goossens.

Originally Walton went to lodge with the Sitwell brothers until he could "find something more permanent" but as he put it himself "I stayed with them for fifteen years." Instead of attending music college, Walton was coached by distinguished musicians, to whom introductions were arranged through the Sitwells. In a letter (22 September 1921) Walton told his mother. "I am very busy at the moment since I am having lessons from Ansermet and Dent". Ernest Ansermet was the principal conductor of Diaghilev's "Les Ballets Russes". He had conducted the premières of Satie's *Parade* and De Falla's *The Three Cornered Hat*. Dent was a distinguished critic and teacher and one of the founders of the International Society for

Contemporary Music in 1923. Ferruccio Busoni was a highly regarded composer and pianist, born in Italy but German by adoption. Dent invited him to London as part of his campaign to restore relations between the Allies and the Central Powers at the end of the Great War. Eugène Goossens came from a prominent musical family. He was a composer and conductor emerging as one of the leaders of the avant-garde; in June 1921 he gave the first concert performance in London of Stravinsky's *The Rite Of Spring* with a virtuoso orchestra. Walton sent Goossens his overture *Dr Syntax*, but a hoped-for performance did not materialise and the score has still not been found.

2 Carlyle Square, Chelsea. Osbert and Sachie moved here from nearby Swan Walk in 1920, taking Walton with them. The grander premises housed their growing collection of contemporary art and served as a base from which to run their campaign to educate the British public.

When Sir George Sitwell bought the Tuscan estate of Montegufoni (in Osbert's name) in 1909 it housed about 300 peasants. "The roof is in splendid order" he wrote to Osbert, "and the drains can't be wrong, as there aren't any."

The Albergo Cappuccini, Amalfi, was a converted monastery. "We all worked in our cells. It was ideal. I had a piano . . . and a room with a view."

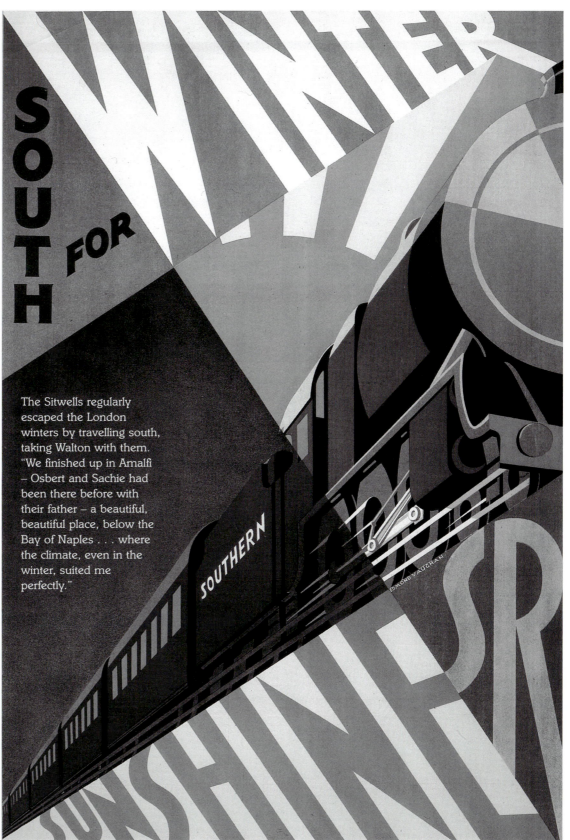

The Sitwells regularly escaped the London winters by travelling south, taking Walton with them. "We finished up in Amalfi – Osbert and Sachie had been there before with their father – a beautiful, beautiful place, below the Bay of Naples . . . where the climate, even in the winter, suited me perfectly."

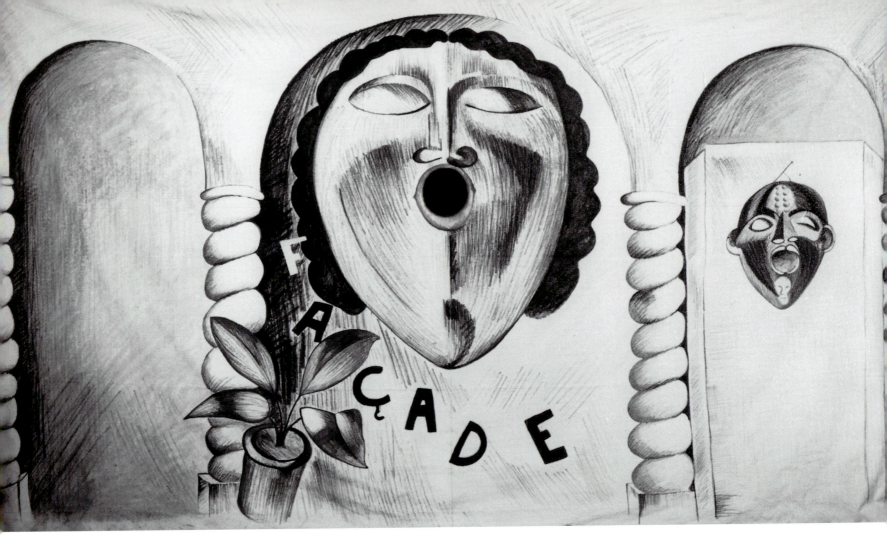

The entertainment *Façade* was first presented in the L-shaped drawing-room of 2 Carlyle Square. The title came from a painter's derogatory reference to Edith Sitwell's experimental poetry: "Very clever, no doubt – but what is she but a façade!" According to Osbert the idea of *Façade* "first entered our minds as the result of certain technical experiments at which my sister had recently been working; experiments in obtaining through the medium of words the rhythm of dance measures such as waltzes, polkas, foxtrots".

Words and music enjoy equal importance in this unique entertainment in which Edith was supported by her brothers: Osbert suggested that the performers should be hidden from view behind a screen, which he commissioned from the sculptor Frank Dobson; Sacheverell located an instrument named the "Sengerphone" through which the poems were declaimed out of the mouth in the centre of the curtain. (Herr Senger, a Swiss opera singer, had invented a fibre trumpet to reinforce his off-stage vocal performance as the dragon Fafner in Wagner's *Siegfried*.)

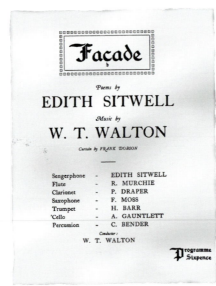

Façade

Poems by
EDITH SITWELL

Music by
W. T. WALTON

Curtain by FRANK DOBSON

Sengerphone	EDITH SITWELL
Flute	R. MURCHIE
Clarionet	P. DRAPER
Saxophone	F. MOSS
Trumpet	H. BARR
'Cello	A. GAUNTLETT
Percussion	C. BENDER

Conductor
W. T. WALTON

Programme
Sixpence

The 1926 performance of *Façade* at the Chenil Galleries, Chelsea, featured from left to right: Osbert Sitwell, Edith Sitwell, Sacheverell Sitwell, Walton and the second reciter Neil Porter (holding the Sengerphone).

Publicity was a vital weapon in the Sitwells' war against the Philistines . . . The artistic intentions behind *Façade* were not in doubt, but the Sitwells were equally aware of the value of notoriety. They were the talk of the town in 1923 when *Façade* was given its first public performance at the Aeolian Hall.

METRICS THROUGH THE MEGAPHONE.

—AND THE SITWELLS   WHY DID THEY DO IT ?   *Specially drawn for the Orbit by Tom Titt*

Left: The front room at 2 Carlyle Square featured a huge bowl of press cuttings on its central table.

Above: The Sitwells as the butt of satire. Mr Tubby Edlin introduces the Brothers Child & Miss Maisie Gray as "The Swiss Family Whittlebot" in Noel Coward's 1925 revue *London's Calling*. The Sitwells shunned Coward for years because of "the impertinence"; Walton thought the skit very funny.

Savoy Medleys

Constant Lambert (1905–1951) became one of Walton's important champions and collaborators. He was equally gifted as composer, conductor and critic and shared with Walton a love of popular music. He became the foremost interpreter of the Walton–Sitwell *Façade*. According to Osbert Sitwell, to whom he introduced himself at the age of seventeen, Lambert was already "a prodigy of intelligence and learning, and gifted with that particularly individual outlook and sense of humour which, surely, were born in him and are impossible to acquire".

Debroy Somers and The Savoy Orpheans, 1923. Walton was introduced to Somers through a friend of Osbert Sitwell's, who was a director of the Savoy Hotel. "In the early days I did do . . . some arrangements for that dance band . . . and tried to write those sorts of tunes, but I wasn't slick enough, somehow. They were more occupied with the 'current' hits to bother very much about my somewhat clumsy efforts . . . I used to be allowed a free tea. Quite a help in those days."

Had his work been accepted, it might have been broadcast on one of the regular Thursday evening relays from the Savoy Hotel Ballroom by the new British Broadcasting Company, whose offices were around the corner at Savoy Hill.

The jazz singer Florence Mills, known as "The Sweet Little Songbird". Her first appearance in London was in the *1923 Revue* of the theatrical impresario C.B. Cochran. Walton's new friend Constant Lambert was a fervent admirer: he had a penchant for exotic women. Black musicians were very much in vogue; a party wasn't a party without one.

Walton bought his suits second hand from Moss Bros.

Above: "The Jazz Age", decorative artwork from a 1923 brochure for Debroy Somers and The Savoy Orpheans Band.

Little is known about Walton's emotional life at this period, but in 1923 he certainly enjoyed a love affair with Zena Naylor, the illegitimate daughter of a Lord. "My Zena! How I wish I could kiss you now but I am sure you know I am doing it in spirit. If not, I send them by wireless from the top of the Eiffel Tower × × × ×." He was en route for Salzburg to hear his String Quartet at the first ISCM Festival. Zena was described by a contemporary as "pretty in a Pekinese-type way, witty and amusing. But she had that quality that destroys so many: she was extremely romantic and always in love. The real love of her life was, I think, Eugène Goossens." When the gossip circulated that she had been discovered *in flagrante* on a sofa with a member of the Black Birds jazz singers (under a Botticelli painting which hung in her father's drawing-room), Walton's ardour cooled. This may explain his decision to destroy "in a fit of disgust" around this time a large-scale work for two pianos, jazz band and symphony orchestra, tentatively entitled *Fantasia Concertante*.

Syncopated rhythm at the Savoy Hotel.

The Paul Whiteman Band. Walton and Lambert heard it at the London Hippodrome. A classically trained musician, Whiteman commissioned *Rhapsody In Blue* from George Gershwin in 1924.

I.

Walton in 1925.
Line drawing by
Christopher Wood.

Walton's First String Quartet was premièred at the International Society of Contemporary Music's 1923 gathering in Salzburg. Osbert Sitwell recalled that "after all the best string quartets in Europe had been playing, these poor good English girls [the McCullagh Quartet] dressed in turquoise tulle put up an abominable performance, added to which the cellist – this you would hardly believe – got the tip of the prong of the cello into the thing that worked a trapdoor above which she was sitting and began to go down! The audience rocked and even she 'came up smiling'."

Alban Berg (1885–1935), left, photographed with his lifesize 1910 portrait, painted by his mentor Arnold Schoenberg. Walton met Berg in Salzburg in 1923 after the Austrian composer had heard the première of Walton's String Quartet. When they went together to meet Schoenberg; Walton noted that the great man was not above using the piano when he composed.

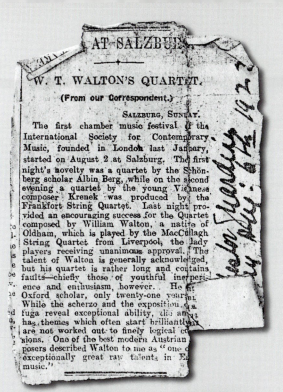

AT-SALZBURG

W. T. WALTON'S QUARTET.

(From our Correspondent.)

SALZBURG, SUNDAY.

The first chamber music festival of the International Society for Contemporary Music, founded in London last January, started on August 2 at Salzburg. The first night's novelty was a quartet by the Schönberg scholar Albin Berg, while on the second evening a quartet by the young Viennese composer Krenek was produced by the Frankfort String Quartet. Last night provided an encouraging success for the Quartet composed by William Walton, a native of Oldham, which is played by the MacCullagh String Quartet from Liverpool, the lady players receiving unanimous approval. The talent of Walton is generally acknowledged, but his quartet is rather long and contains faults—chiefly those of youthful inexperience and enthusiasm, however. He is an Oxford scholar, only twenty-one years old. While the scherzo and the exposition of a fuga reveal exceptional ability, the andante has themes which often start brilliantly, but are not worked out to finely logical conclusions. One of the best modern Austrian composers described Walton to me as "one of exceptionally great raw talents in English music."

Manchester Guardian,
6 August 1923.

Friends and contemporaries

The cover of Walton's Piano Quartet, one of his first published works. Completed in 1919, it was published in 1924 by Stainer & Bell Ltd and paid for by the Carnegie Trust under a scheme dedicated to encourage young British composers; the adjudicators included Ralph Vaughan Williams. The manuscript had been "lost in the post" between Italy and England for two years. Walton presented this copy to George Gershwin when they met in London in May 1925.

Vladimir Dukelsky (1903–1969) a.k.a. Vernon Duke, Russian–American composer. He introduced Walton to his friend Gershwin. Dukelsky wrote a ballet for Diaghilev, but his best known music was for the play *Cabin In The Sky* and the evergreen *April in Paris*.

George Gershwin (1898–1937). His *Rhapsody In Blue* was all the rage. "I had been an admirer of his brilliant and captivating tunes", Walton recalled; "he was in the middle of writing his Piano Concerto in F, and I was hypnotized by his fabulous piano playing and his melodic gift."

Hyam "Bumps" Greenbaum (1901–1942), violinist, conductor and composer. A close friend of Walton, he married Eugène Goossens's sister, Sidonie, the harpist. From 1930 to 1934 he was music director to C.B. Cochran and later the first conductor of the BBC Television Orchestra. He orchestrated Walton's first film score *Escape Me Never.*

Philip Heseltine (1894–1930) (a.k.a. the composer Peter Warlock). According to Osbert Sitwell, Walton "entertained a high regard for him and greatly enjoyed his conversation and together with Constant would go down to spend convivial evenings with him in Kent . . . whence the two young composers would return very late, with footsteps faltering through the now uncertain immensity of night . . . ". However, Walton's wife suggests that he didn't like Heseltine very much: he "led a tormented life, indulged in black magic practices, and eventually committed suicide".

Bernard van Dieren (1887–1936). According to Osbert Sitwell "both his livelihood and his health were precarious and the promotion of his music was largely dependent on the efforts of a handful of devotees" – among them Walton and Sacheverell Sitwell, who planned a recital of his songs while they were still at Oxford.

Angus Morrison (1902–1989), concert pianist of broad sensitivities and a close friend of Walton and Lambert.

Lytton Strachey (1880–1932), a prominent member of the Bloomsbury Group best known for his brief lives of *Eminent Victorians*. Walton wrote the incidental music for Strachey's *The Son Of Heaven* in 1925. The play, about the Boxer Rising, was universally panned and quickly disappeared. "Easily the dullest play we have walked out of since Arnold Bennett's *The Bright Island*" (wrote the critic of *The Curtain*).

The dancers Serge Lifar and Alexandra Danilova with Lord Berners on the set of the Diaghilev ballet *The Triumph of Neptune*. Sacheverell Sitwell concocted the story, mixing elements of Victorian pantomime and modern surrealism. Berners composed the music; the choreographer was George Balanchine. "We saw at the Lyceum last night the beginnings of a British Ballet" claimed Hannen Swaffer in the *Daily Express* (4 December 1926). Berners, wrote Osbert Sitwell, was "a sort of missionary of the arts, bringing a touch of unwanted fun into many a dreary life". Walton was hauled in to help orchestrate *The Triumph of Neptune*. "I've been so terribly busy this last month" (Walton wrote to his mother), "I've had to orchestrate four large numbers for Berners's ballet". In the interval of the performance Walton conducted the pit orchestra in a suite he had made of music from *Façade*. "Quite a surprise my being asked to do it . . . unfortunately I received nothing for it, but it is well worth doing for the experience."

Serge Diaghilev (1872–1929). The great ballet impresario was a regular visitor to the Sitwell house in Carlyle Square. In 1925 he commissioned Constant Lambert to compose the score for the ballet *Romeo and Juliet*. Walton's hopes of a similar commission were dashed in the same year. Diaghilev listened to a ballet score Walton had composed the previous winter, but dismissed it, content to observe, with his customary acumen, that the composer would surely go on to write better things.

Walton with his publisher Hubert Foss (1899–1953). Sartorially, Walton was still at the mercy of the ill-fitting "seconds" from Moss Bros.

Behind the scenes Foss worked tirelessly to promote Oxford University Press's rapidly expanding catalogue of contemporary English music. However his career faltered during the war years and he died – of a stroke – tragically young.

Dora Stevens (Mrs Hubert Foss). With her husband at the piano, she gave the first performance of Walton's *Three Songs* at the Wigmore Hall in 1932. All three, "Old Sir Faulk", "Daphne" and "Through Gilded Trellises" are adaptations of numbers from *Façade*.

The piano duet transcription of *Portsmouth Point* was the first of Walton's compositions to be published by OUP.

Thomas Rowlandson's etching *Portsmouth Point* was the inspiration for Walton's first surviving composition for symphony orchestra. The music was premièred in Zurich in June 1926 as part of that year's ISCM Festival.

Cecil Beaton's "Jazz Age" portrait of Walton.

Siesta was dedicated to Stephen Tennant, (1906–1987), the fourth son of Lord and Lady Glenconner. Walton conducted the first performance at the Aeolian Hall in 1926. He also made this arrangement for piano duet. The original manuscript has disappeared.

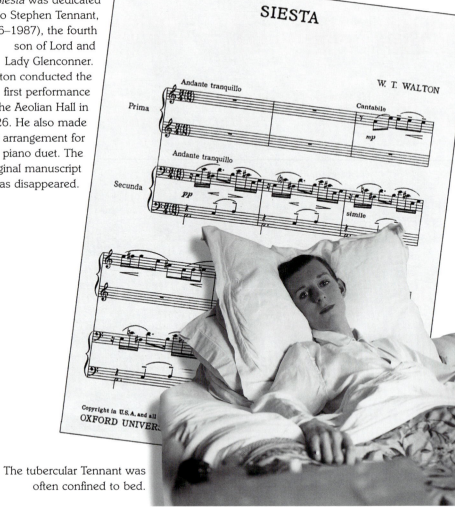

The tubercular Tennant was often confined to bed.

Conversation at the Daye House by Rex Whistler. Edith Olivier (left) was a prominent society hostess who lived at the Daye House in Quidhampton, near Salisbury. With her are the young aesthete Lord David Cecil, Lady Ottoline Morrell and (at right) the artist and designer Rex Whistler. Edith asked Walton's opinion about a new piano; he chose the model on the left-hand side of this picture and often used it when composing.

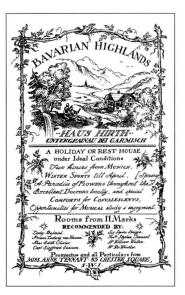

Rex Whistler's design for an advertisement for Haus Hirth, endorsed by Walton and others in Tennant's circle.

"The Bright Young Things" dressed as stylish shepherds for a home movie shot at Tennant's home, Wilsford Manor, in 1927. Left to right: Zita Jungmann, Walton, Cecil Beaton, Stephen Tennant, Georgia Sitwell, Baby Jungmann and Rex Whistler. Walton carried a torch for Baby.

Haus Hirth, Untergrainau, in the foothills of the Bavarian Alps, where Tennant was sent for rest cures. Siegfried Sassoon paid for Walton to accompany the flamboyant Tennant on trips abroad "to keep an eye on him".

Sassoon and Tennant. Sassoon was one of Walton's most generous financial supporters. The Sitwell brothers provided Walton with a bed and introductions but they had little cash to spare and Sassoon often bailed him out. Sassoon fell head over heels for Tennant. Their tempestuous affair ended in heartbreak and divided their friends.

Imma von Doernberg (1901–1947). Strikingly beautiful, she was born into an aristocratic German family and was distantly related to British and Dutch royalty. In 1923 she married Baron Hans-Karl von Doernberg, 26 years her senior. He died less than a year later. Her cousin, HRH Princess Alice, Countess of Athlone, described her as "the most alive and buoyant person imaginable". Walton fell deeply in love with her.

Top right: Printed score of Walton's *Sinfonia Concertante*. The first performance was given in 1928. The three movements were dedicated respectively to Osbert, Edith and Sacheverell Sitwell.

Main picture, right: The novelist Evelyn Waugh wrote that the Sitwells "radiated an aura of high spirits, elegance, impudence, unpredictability, above all sheer enjoyment . . . they declared war on dullness". But by the end of the 1920s the siblings were inevitably going their separate ways.

Right: David Horner, known in the Sitwell circle as "Blossom". His relationship with Osbert precipitated Walton's departure from Carlyle Square.

Centre right: Pavel Fyodorovitch Tchelitchew ("Pavlik" to his friends), homosexual White Russian painter. Edith moved to Paris to be near him. She became his "muse", but eventually he broke her heart. She wrote later that their friendship was punctuated by "rows of unbelievable ferocity".

Far right: Georgia Sitwell (née Doble). She was the daughter of a Canadian banker. She and Sachie fell in love and married in Paris in 1925. Walton was best man. According to Edith's biographer "Edith and Osbert were taken aback by the idea of Sachie – or of any of them – marrying anyone at all."

Portrait of the composer as a young man.
William Walton circa 1928, by Elizabeth Corcorran.

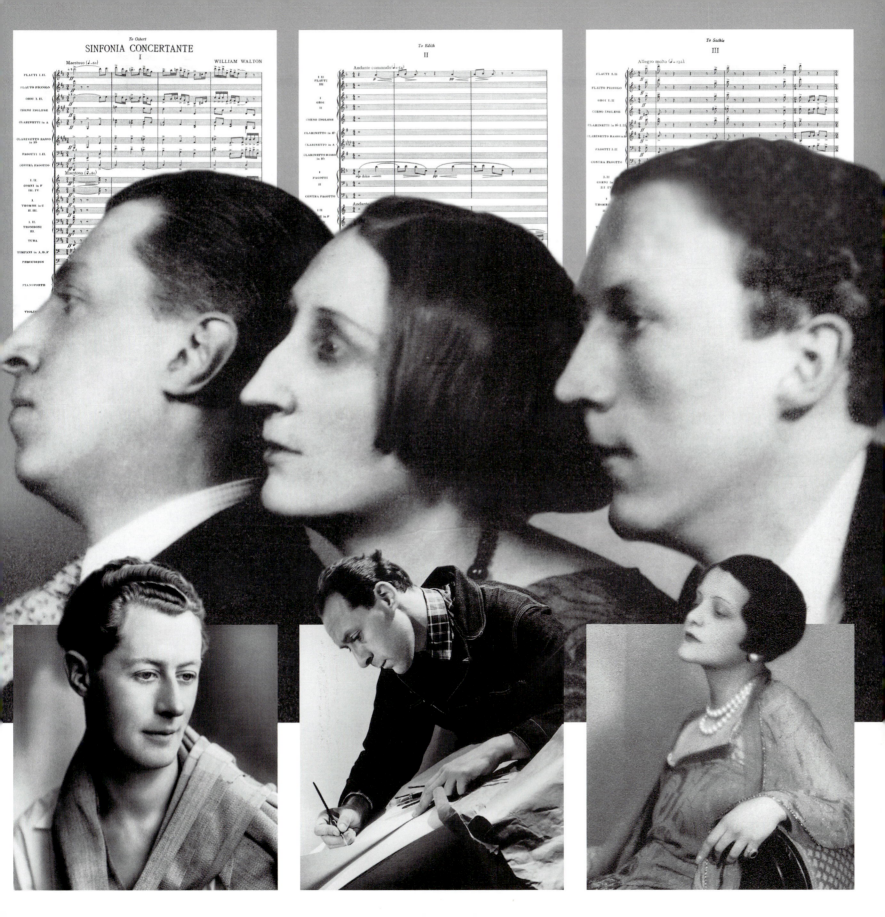

> "I was a
> scrounger ...
> and scrounge
> I did for a very
> long time."

SECRETS OF A YOUNG BRITISH COMPOSER'S INCOME.

THE GRAND OPERA BATTLE.

By GORDON BECKLES,
"Daily Express" Music Critic.

OPERATIC battles are usually comic affairs, but—unless wiser counsels prevail—the curtain will shortly rise on an operatic battle that is anything but funny.

Sir Thomas Beecham seems to have decided to launch his Imperial League of Opera in London next May—concurrent with the opening of the Covent Garden season—on the grounds that the two seasons will be mutually beneficial.

But can two seasons running at the same time be anything but a gamble? Yesterday, as I passed Covent Garden, I saw them unloading the properties used on their first provincial tour; a tour which, Colonel Eustace Blois told his company, has proved highly successful. They are likely to have lost far less money than during the big May season in London.

Both Covent Garden and the Imperial League of Opera are possessed of large funds of money; and both are quite willing to fight for premier place.

It is a situation which allows of no compromise. If Sir Thomas Beecham and Lieut.-Colonel Eustace Blois are really sincere and determined in their expressed desire to give England a permanent operatic organisation, they will —sooner or later—have to amalgamate. Why not now?

Covent Garden has the theatre, the machine, the commercial instinct; the League has youth, an immense following, ideas—and Sir Thomas Beecham.

Lambert's "Rio Grande."

There are only two composers who have anything to say in music just now.

One of them is Constant Lambert, whose "Rio Grande" is as fine a piece of work as this syncopated age has heard; a hauntingly vivid impression of a remarkably lovely poem by one Sacheverell Sitwell.

Sir Hamilton Harty played the piano for its performance at the Queen's Hall the other night, while his Hallé Orchestra—or such part of it as was necessary—played under Mr. Lambert's baton.

Just before the music began the other young-man-who-has-something-to-say came up and said: "Don't miss a second of this. It's great. Much better than I have ever written. . . ."

That man was Mr. William Walton.

Copied The Scores.

"Willie" Walton is a Lancashire man, not yet thirty years of age.

At the age of ten he won a probationership in Christ Church Cathedral

MR. WILLIAM WALTON.

at Oxford, and six years later became an undergraduate.

When he was seventeen he had passed the "Mus. Bac." examinations.

And, to-day he is internationally famous, although most Englishmen only know his name in connection with a composition called "Portsmouth Point."

This work has been played all over the world since it was written in 1925, its career having started in Zurich during the 1926 session of the International Music Festival.

A Clerical Task.

When he heard that it was really going to be played there, Walton sat down after his months of composition, and started to write out the sixty score parts needed for its performance.

The clerical task of copying out the parts for the orchestra took him six weeks.

But as the work was a great success he did not mind; besides, a firm of publishers came along and offered to participate in his glory on a cash basis.

So then Mr. Walton became a moneyed man—as far as his music was concerned.

He received a royalty on every copy of "Portsmouth Point" sold—not lent—and also half the Performing Right Society's fee, the other half, quite rightly, going to his publisher.

Thus "Portsmouth Point" journeyed around the world, enjoying prosperity under the most favourable financial circumstances.

Although it had taken some nine months of his time, Mr. Walton rested assured that his work had genuine merits which were really being appreciated; in a sense, being his first success, it was a life work.

£20 Profits.

Four years have passed since "Portsmouth Point" first started on its travels as one of the most popular English works of the post-war decade.

It has earned its composer nearly £20 so far, but he hopes that its recent gramophone recording and the fact that the Chicago Symphony is touring it in America will possibly increase his profits.

I recite these facts because they may be of interest to the Socialist M.P.s who

have spent so much time concocting the Musical Copyright Bill.

This, you may remember, is the comic document which would limit the fee on all pieces of music to twopence!

From his greatest and most-played piece of work Mr. William Walton has earned, in all, nearly £20. If it had been under the proposed law he might have earned nearly 20s.

Some people say that the Musical Copyright Bill is a very necessary piece of legislation . . .

B.B.C.'s Initiative.

Every other country but his own has produced Walton's works for the first time, so he does not worry. Early next year he is to conduct his works at a big concert in Berlin. "Portsmouth Point" will be featured, with "Sinfonia Concerta," "Siesta," and his suite from "Façade," while Paul Hindemith himself will play the new "Viola Concerto."

Meantime Walton is going abroad to execute the first commission ever given by the British Broadcasting Corporation to a British composer!

He has chosen "Belshazzar's Feast" as a subject, but has uncertain ideas as to how his work will form itself, save that it will be built around a Sitwell narrative.

Broadcasting Flaws.

Some people seem to detect a hyper-critical attitude in my remarks towards the B.B.C. This is detection of the wrong kind. It is wrong because I know—and will say—that the B.B.C. has set music on its feet in this country. True, it could have set it on its feet more solidly, but for what it has done may we all be truly thankful. . . .

But I often feel, when a Beethoven

—And Why Not?

"In the arrangement of the programmes, the claims of modern British and contemporary composers will not be overlooked, and in this connection it will be of interest to note that a reading committee of qualified musicians is being appointed by the directors to recommend new works of merit, irrespective of School, Race, or Creed."—From the programme of the London Concert Orchestra.

symphony is in progress at the Queen's Hall, that seven-tenths of the listeners-in will probably have turned off their sets in disgust after the first five minutes, prompted either by ignorance of the work that is being played or by mechanical flaws.

Walton's "Belshazzar's Feast" will be accompanied by an explanatory narrative that will, at the same time, be an integral part of the work itself.

And it will avoid as far as possible too much string, oboe, and horn music, none of which "come over" the ether in decent style.

Daily Express, 7 December 1929.

CHAPTER 4

A DECADE OF MASTERPIECES

1929–1939

"At last a real voice"

GUIDO ADLER, GERMAN CRITIC

Walton at Ascona, circa 1932.
The photograph was probably taken
by Imma von Doernberg.

ACCORDING TO STEPHEN TENNANT, who knew them both well, Walton was "adored" by Christabel McLaren, the first woman other than his "adopted sister" Edith Sitwell to whom he dedicated one of his compositions. She was a close friend of Osbert Sitwell. Since the work in question, the dark-hued Viola Concerto, was the most overtly romantic music he ever wrote, one might suppose a love story behind the dedication but it seems they were just very good friends. She was the daughter of a former head of Scotland Yard and became Lady Aberconway in 1934 when her husband, Henry McLaren succeeded to a peerage. Eleven years older than Walton and the mistress of Samuel Courtauld, the industrialist, art collector and philanthropist, Christabel was the same age as Osbert and a particularly vivacious member of his circle. He later described her unflatteringly as "a gossip, a tale-bearer and a trouble-maker" but Walton was forever indebted to her for inspiring Mrs Elizabeth Courtauld to make him a bequest of £500 per annum for life, a godsend for somebody whose annual royalty income was less than £100 and whose need to seek help from his friends had begun to rival Mozart's.

The Viola Concerto was composed in Italy in the winter of 1928–29. Another member of the Sitwell circle, Sir Thomas Beecham, had suggested the idea of writing a work for a neglected solo instrument recently brought into prominence through the efforts of the virtuoso performer Lionel Tertis. The compositional hesitations experienced earlier in the decade had gone: Walton hit his stride within days of reaching Amalfi and felt he had discovered a new and eloquent vein. "My style is changing", he wrote to his pianist friend Angus Morrison, "it is becoming more melodious and mature." To Sassoon he confided that the concerto was "by far my best effort up to now". When the ailing Tertis committed the unpardonable gaffe of declining to give the première of the concerto at a Promenade Concert, the BBC sent an SOS to the composer Paul Hindemith, whom Walton had met at the 1923 ISCM Festival at Salzburg. Hindemith still played regularly in a string quartet and despite his rather dry tone the performance was a triumph. Tertis ate humble pie concerning the work's alleged incomprehensibility and thereafter played it with great authority. Ernest Newman, the most influential critic of the day, declared Walton to be "of quite exceptional gifts . . . the best of our younger composers", he continued "are now writing as if the malign influence of the late M. Diaghilev and others had never been."

1929 was a significant year for Walton. Even before the Viola Concerto's première, the BBC approached him with the first commission ever offered to a composer to write a work specifically for broadcasting. This was to be the oratorio *Belshazzar's Feast*. Walton eventually felt obliged to withdraw from the commission when his sonic concept assumed such grandiose proportions that radio engineering techniques (in those pioneer days) would have been unable to do it justice. Also in 1929, the Decca Record Company made the first recording of Walton's music, a set of two 78 rpm disks containing eleven numbers from *Façade* narrated by

Constant Lambert and Miss Sitwell herself. For many *aficionados* they were the finest of all the work's many star interpreters.

With musical maturity and public recognition came signs of personal self-confidence: at the turn of the decade Walton fell in love, and with a woman of his own age, Imma von Doernberg. Many years later he confided to his wife, Susana, that being emotionally a late developer he had had only one real relationship before Imma: perhaps he was thinking of Zena Naylor (see page 51). Imma was the daughter of a German prince, a distant cousin of the Countess of Athlone and the recent widow of a baron much older than herself who died within a year of their marriage. Titles meant little in the Weimar Republic, however – although Walton's society friends were impressed – and the baroness's modest private means were cruelly depleted by the inflation that destroyed the German economy at the beginning of the 1930s. The beautiful and vivacious Imma nevertheless made Walton happy during the years when he completed *Belshazzar's Feast* and the opening movements of his First Symphony. Siegfried Sassoon described her as being "pretty, sweet, lively and courageous . . . with a tall, graceful figure". Their letters from Ascona, on Lake Maggiore, describe their quiet domestic life together and hint at why Walton would one day choose to settle for ever in a landscape that was the antithesis of Oldham. He loved to take out a canoe and paddle on the lake. "It is heavenly here", he wrote to Sassoon, "and I am immensely happy" – not a sentiment one reads often in his correspondence.

Belshazzar's Feast was longer in gestation than the Viola Concerto; Walton was stuck for many months at the point in the oratorio where the pagan Babylonians praise the god of gold. His

Freifrau Imma von Doernberg, "W.W.'s baroness".

eventual solution was a glittering march that is first cousin to the Pomp and Circumstance of Elgar in his ceremonial mode. The oratorio's première was given at the Leeds Festival of 1931; another sagacious suggestion from Sir Thomas Beecham led to the incorporation of two brass bands to illuminate the joyful injunction to the liberated Jewish slaves to "blow up the trumpet in the new moon". This was Walton's first work for solo voice, choir and orchestra and he carried it off with astonishing assurance. The pathos of the refugees' chorus, "By the waters of Babylon" is every bit as eloquent as the equivalent passage in Verdi's opera *Nabucco*. The eerie orchestration heralding the solo baritone's account of the mysterious writing on the wall can still send shivers down the spine, while the barbaric glitter of pagan revelries had not been so clamorously evoked since Richard Strauss's *Salome*. Neville Cardus summed up *Belshazzar's Feast* as "a clear case of red-hot conception instinctively finding the right and equally red-hot means of expression".

Had he been an Italian, Walton would immediately have turned to composing an opera (as he was urged to do by Ernest Newman) but England had no operatic tradition and early in 1932 Sir Hamilton Harty commissioned him to write a symphony for the Hallé Orchestra. (Harty took the commission with him when he moved to the London Symphony Orchestra.) The work was conceived during the years of economic and political turmoil prior to Hitler's rise to power in 1933. Walton had learned about Germany's problems at first hand from Imma and after talking to Swiss banker friends he wrote despairingly to Sassoon urging him to transfer his funds to safe Switzerland before

Britain's economy collapsed. He claimed to have no interest in politics but it is difficult not to read something of the world's tensions into the symphony, particularly its powerful opening movement.

The symphony expresses a personal crisis, too. The relationship with the highly-strung Imma von Doernberg became troubled. She had shared Walton's triumph at the 1931 Leeds Festival and helped translate the text into German but wrote soon after of her sadness at parting from William, expressing doubts as to whether it would be possible to continue the relationship. Mrs Courtauld's bequest enabled Walton to spend more time with her in Ascona in the spring of 1932 but Imma's health had deteriorated and – as he wrote – "such things as symphonies have fallen far into the background". Walton stirred his stumps nevertheless when he learned that he was to be in competition with England's greatest symphonist – the BBC had commissioned a Third Symphony from Elgar – and two movements of Walton's new work were finished by Christmas. Two months later a vexed Hamilton Harty wrote to the publisher: "Why don't you go over to Switzerland and wrest poor W.W.'s Baroness away from him so he can stop making overtures to her and do a symphony for me instead." It wasn't a bad joke and was prophetically close to the mark: Walton wrote an acerbic Scherzo marked "con malizia" (with malice) to precede the slow movement. The latter was perhaps the most eloquent, heartfelt and touching music he ever composed, but he then experienced another of his paralysing writer's blocks, in the course of which he finally broke with Imma. In the light of the undoubted warmth of their relationship, it is rather sad to learn that she left him for a Hungarian doctor, complaining that Walton had become impotent; she eventually married an affluent homosexual, Capt Neal McEacharn, thus acquiring the British passport which enabled her to live in Canada and Australia during the war. She died of leukaemia, aged only 46.

Musical history was made in November 1934 when the LSO performed a new *Unfinished Symphony* – by William Walton. Unable to complete the work to his satisfaction, the composer had deferred the première several times until the orchestra would brook no further delay. Afterwards Walton was a nervous wreck but he soon found his feet again, helped by a new and most unlikely relationship with a woman twenty-two years his elder, Alice Wimborne. Like her predecessor in Walton's affection Alice was (as William enjoyed pointing out) a baroness – good-looking and amazingly youthful for her age. A blue-blooded, fun-loving, piano-playing, imperious arts patroness, she was the wife of one of the richest men in Britain, Ivor Guest, second Viscount Wimborne, and another old friend of the Sitwells. Osbert had recently come out of the closet and set up home with his handsome young friend David Horner; he disapproved of Walton's liaison with somebody from his own intimate circle and the composer was no longer welcome at Carlyle Square.

In 1935 Walton bought a small house in South Eaton Place, Belgravia, with the money he earned composing film music. His first experience of this lucrative field was *Escape Me Never,* starring the Austrian actress Elisabeth Bergner and directed by her Hungarian husband Paul Czinner. Frederick Ashton was to arrange the choreography. "They want us to write bad Russian ballet music," Walton whispered to Ashton when they met the producers: "let's do it!" After this enjoyable diversion he returned to his symphony and Alice's steadying influence enabled him to bring it to a triumphant conclusion. The finale was not a tacked-on afterthought: much of it had been sketched before the writer's block set in. Lambert now suggested topping it off with a fugue. Walton is said to have studied a two-page article on the subject in Grove's Dictionary before composing a magnificent example of the genre that must have warmed the hearts of his former professors at Oxford. The symphony's long-deferred première was, in Walton's own phrase, "the climax of my youth". A respected fellow composer, John Ireland, said it was "the work of the most vital and original genius in Europe".

We can record only briefly the lighter aspects of what was arguably the most fruitful decade in Walton's creative life. In 1931 Constant Lambert conducted the hugely entertaining ballet based on movements from *Façade* which Walton had earlier transformed into concert music for a symphony orchestra, omitting the Sitwell poems. The choreographer was Frederick Ashton, with whom he worked again in 1935 on *The First Shoot,* a ten-minute ballet with a story line by Osbert Sitwell and costumes by Cecil Beaton, part of a lavish Silver Jubilee Year review produced by England's closest rival to the late Serge Diaghilev, Mr C.B. Cochran. Walton's career as a film composer flourished with his first Shakespeare film, *As You Like It,* in 1936. Then came *Dreaming Lips* and *A Stolen Life* – attractive, lightweight cinematic projects which he dispatched swiftly and effectively, with none of the hang-ups associated with the composition of his concert music. Less ephemeral but even more lucrative in the long run was *Crown Imperial,* the stirring march he composed in 1937 for the coronation of King George VI. Later that year a new cantata for chorus and orchestra, *In Honour of the City of London* – an incongruous title for a work commissioned by the city of Leeds – failed to repeat the success of *Belshazzar's Feast.* An undeniably colourful portrait of mediaeval London, "the flower of cities all", it suffers from an absence of dramatic thrust.

In 1939 Walton completed the beautiful Violin Concerto commissioned three years previously by the leading virtuoso of the pre-war age, Jascha Heifetz. A plan to give its première at the New York World Fair had to be cancelled because the British Council failed to check on Heifetz's availability; instead the first performance took place in December 1939 in the relative obscurity of Cleveland, Ohio, under the direction of Artur Rodzinski. The concerto was dedicated to Heifetz, who paid only £300 ($1500) for two years exclusivity on the work. The performer's virtuosity is exploited in many scintillating bravura passages but emotionally the music expresses the depth of Walton's feelings for Alice Wimborne. She had a hand in its composition, too. To help him recuperate after a bilateral hernia operation she installed him in the magnificent Villa Cimbrone, overlooking the Mediterranean above Ravello. He settled down to compose and she got very cross, he reported to his publisher, "if I mucked about". Perhaps he sensed that this was to be the last romantic idyll in a world that was soon to turn sour. In June 1939, when he was in New York to work with Heifetz on the final revisions of his Violin Concerto, he gave a prophetic interview to the *New York Times*: "To-day's white hope is tomorrow's black sheep. These days it is very sad for a composer to grow old – unless, that is, he grows old enough to witness a revival of his work. I seriously advise all sensitive composers to die at the age of 37. [His age exactly] I know: I've gone through the first halcyon periods, and am just about ripe for my critical damnation."

Another snap from Ascona.
Walton was composing his First
Symphony and "immensely happy".

Lionel Tertis (1876–1975), the British viola virtuoso for whom Walton intended his Viola Concerto. "It took me time to realise what a tower of strength in the literature of the viola is this concerto", Tertis wrote later. "With shame and contrition I admit that when the composer offered me the first performance, I declined it . . . The innovations in his musical language which now seem so logical and so truly in the mainstream of music then struck me as far-fetched."

Paul Hindemith (1895–1963), the outstanding German composer, was also a professional viola player and at short notice gave the première of Walton's concerto at the Queen's Hall.

Programme for the first performance of the Viola Concerto on 3 October 1929.

PROMENADE
CONCERTS

PROGRAMME

*THIRTY-FIFTH
SEASON*

THURSDAY, 3 OCTOBER
1929

BRITISH BROADCASTING CORPORATION

Sir Edward Elgar (1857–1934). Walton met Elgar only once, when they both conducted at the 1932 Three Choirs Festival. Elgar was reported by the critic Basil Maine to have "paced up and down behind the orchestral gallery during the performance of the [viola] concerto 'deploring that such music should be thought fit for a stringed instrument'".

Christabel McLaren, sketched by Augustus John. She became Lady Aberconway when her husband inherited the baronetcy in 1934. She was an intimate friend of Samuel Courtauld, with whom she shared a passion for modern painting.

Samuel and Elizabeth Courtauld. They were noted supporters of the arts. He donated valuable paintings to the Tate Gallery and later endowed the Courtauld Institute. In 1928 she inaugurated an important series of symphony concerts conducted by Malcolm Sargent.

LOSS TO THE MUSICAL WORLD
Mrs. Courtauld's Energy and Hard Work
By the death, on Christmas Day, of Mrs. Courtauld, music loses one of its most valuable and generous supporters.

Elizabeth Courtauld died in 1931. Her will benefitted a number of struggling artists, among them Walton, who received a £500 annuity which changed his life.

The manuscript of the Viola Concerto is headed with the dedication "To Christabel".

LEEDS MUSICAL FESTIVAL 1931

THURSDAY EVENING

October 8th, at Seven-Thirty

Conductor:

DR. MALCOLM SARGENT

VAUGHAN WILLIAMS'
SONG FOR CHORUS & ORCHESTRA
"TOWARD THE UNKNOWN REGION"

BACH'S CONCERTO IN D MINOR
FOR TWO VIOLINS AND ORCHESTRA

ERIC FOGG'S CHORAL WORK (NEW)
"THE SEASONS" (Conducted by the Composer)

WILLIAM WALTON'S CHORAL WORK
(NEW) "BELSHAZZAR'S FEAST"

RIMSKY-KORSAKOV'S
"ANTAR" SYMPHONY

PRICE - TWO SHILLINGS

Cover page for the Leeds Musical Festival programme for the première of *Belshazzar's Feast*.

"BELSHAZZAR'S FEAST."

Composer Cheered by Leeds Audience.

Sensational Success.

A typically laudatory headline in *The Yorkshire Post*, 9 October 1931.

LEEDS FESTIVAL: DR. MALCOLM SARGENT IN ACTION.

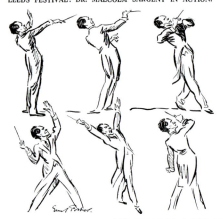

Caricatures of Malcolm Sargent (1895–1967), who conducted the first performance of *Belshazzar's Feast*. Walton's sometimes uneasy professional relationship with Sargent continued until the conductor's death.

Dennis Noble, leading English baritone, first appeared at Covent Garden in 1924 and in 1931 received rave reviews for his interpretation of the dramatic solo in *Belshazzar's Feast*.

Leeds Town Hall, where *Belshazzar's Feast* was premièred. Not for the last time, the scale of the original BBC commission was overtaken by Walton's creative ambition. The Director of the Leeds Festival, Sir Thomas Beecham, encouraged Walton to write for large forces: "Why not throw in a couple of brass bands? No one will ever hear the piece again." The prophecy proved unduly pessimistic. Sir Andrew Davis was in charge of a performance filmed for BBC Television in 1999.

BELSHAZZAR'S FEAST

for Mixed Choir, Baritone Solo and Orchestra

by WILLIAM WALTON

Text selected and arranged from the Holy Bible by
OSBERT SITWELL

German Translation by
Beryl de Zoete
and
Baronin Imma Doernberg

Belshazzar's Feast originated from a BBC commission to write a radio work for "a small chorus, small orchestra of not exceeding fifteen and soloist". Looking for a theme with popular appeal, Osbert Sitwell proposed the story of Belshazzar's Feast in Babylon, maintaining it was a subject "everyone would know about". Walton, for one, didn't. Christabel McLaren helped Sitwell assemble the biblical text from the book of Daniel, the Psalms, Isaiah and the Book of Revelations. Walton's friend Imma von Doernberg worked on the German translation.

Willie and I had two more nice days at London, but the parting is always the most painful decision to set forth, specially now, when the circumstances are more and more against us and it might even be such a long time before we see each other again — I wished I could do more for Willie but I have the feeling that fate is at the end against the fact that our two lives settle down together. —

Letter from Imma to Siegfried Sassoon presaging the end of her love affair with Walton. In another letter she thanked Sassoon for his continued financial support: "I am very grateful for all these peaceful months we could spend together, which is entirely due to you! God bless you for it."

To Imma
Freifrau Von Darnberg

SYMPHONY

William Walton

MCMXXXIII

Rex Whistler's design for the frontispiece of Walton's First Symphony dates from 1933 but the symphony was not completed until two years later. In the interim, the symphony's dedicatee, "Imma Freifrau von Darnberg", had left the composer.

Walton and his baroness in Switzerland. They lived together in Ascona on Lake Maggiore. She suffered from an increasingly nervous disposition, exacerbated by the drying up of her allowance from her father at the time of Germany's economic collapse. After dental treatment, Walton reported to Sassoon, she contracted "a ghastly infection"; it spread to her bones and all over her head, causing "fearful pain".

Walton's manuscript for the opening of the symphony's sinister Second Movement. The tempo instruction is "Presto con malizia" (fast with malice).

When the relationship with Imma foundered, Walton experienced a severe case of writer's block. But the London Symphony Orchestra had scheduled the first performance for the 1934 season and conductor Sir Hamilton Harty (who had commissioned the symphony) decided to go ahead despite the composer's inability to produce a final movement. The mental turmoil occasioned by the break-up of his affair with Imma – "jealousy and hatred all mixed up with love" – undoubtedly contributed to this creative impasse but may also be a source of the symphony's colossal emotional power.

I've burnt about 3 finales when I saw that they weren't really leading anywhere or saying anything. For it is, for want of better words, what may be called the emotional & spiritual continuity that is worrying me & not so much the actual notes. (but they are bad enough.)

Letter to Walton's friend and colleague, the composer Patrick Hadley, 9 November 1934.

Alice, Viscountess Wimborne (1880–1948). She and Walton began an affair in 1934. Walton reported it thus: "I changed horses, so to speak . . . Imma left me, and I found beautiful, intelligent Alice. She was very kind, full of all the virtues." She played the piano well and often organised concerts at Wimborne House, her London home.

Lord and Lady Wimborne. They were married in 1902, the year of Walton's birth. As Ivor Guest, he had been a steel magnate who served as Lord Lieutenant of Ireland during the 1916 Troubles. He was made a Viscount at the end of the First World War. The Wimbornes enjoyed what used to be known as an "Edwardian" marriage; Walton got on well with the Viscount. An influential figure in inter-war politics, he inspired the following couplet:

"One must suppose that God knew best,
When he created Ivor Guest."

Mr. Walton's Symphony

LADY WIMBORNE'S party at Wimborne House on Wednesday was something of a novelty. I cannot think of any precedent for a leading London hostess celebrating the first performance of a new symphony with such circumstance.

The composer was Mr. William Walton, the first three movements of whose symphony were performed twice last season. After the entire work had been heard, Mr. Walton received congratulations from Lord Carisbrooke and from at least a hundred others of Lady Wimborne's guests.

Sunday Times, 10 November 1935.

The Wimbornes entertained in grand style. Siegfried Sassoon described one of their parties as "Rome before the Fall". Dora Foss recalled a supper at which "seventeen footmen looked after thirty-five guests". (see also page 84)

The opening page of the long-awaited Finale movement of Walton's Symphony No.1. "The tears were rolling down my cheeks during the Epilogue, as they were down many others!" wrote Hubert Foss to his wife.

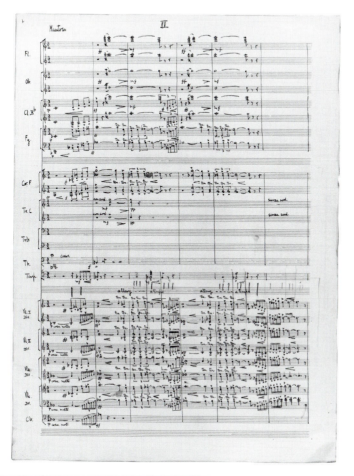

Walton in 1935. In Alice Wimborne's scrapbook for Symphony No. 1 this photograph is described as the first to be seen in the American press. Her family accepted that Alice liked men younger than herself.

The programme for the first performance of the completed Symphony No. 1.

Sir Hamilton Harty (1879–1941), Irish composer and conductor. His long relationship with the Hallé Orchestra ended in acrimony in 1933 and he took with him to the London Symphony Orchestra his commission for the Walton Symphony. It was performed without Finale on 3 December 1934. He also conducted the première of the complete work on 6 November 1935, this time with the BBC Symphony Orchestra. Harty declared the symphony to be the finest work of which he had ever given the première. 73

Poster for the concert on 6 November 1935.

B·B·C
Symphony Concert

WILLIAM WALTON

SYMPHONY No.1

FIRST PERFORMANCE
OF THE COMPLETE WORK

TO-NIGHT AT 8.30
AT 8.30

IN THE QUEEN'S HALL

SOLE LESSEES : MESSRS. CHAPPELL & Co., Ltd.

LANGLEY & SONS, LTD, THE EUSTON PRESS, N.W.1

Right: Portrait of the composer by Howard Coster,
taken at the time of the symphony's composition.

NORTHERN GENIUS

IT is good to be able to acclaim a Northern genius. The new symphony by William Walton, which has received such highly commendatory notices from the critics, is striking proof of the vitality of English music.

THE COMPLETED SYMPHONY

WILLIAM WALTON'S IMPOSING WORK

OVATION FOR YOUNG COMPOSER

BRILLIANT SYMPHONY WRITTEN AT 33

TRIUMPH FOR WILLIAM WALTON

First Symphony Premiere

ENGLISH COMPOSER'S TRIUMPH.

GREAT OVATION AFTER A FIRST PERFORMANCE.

Young Composer's Triumph

A NEW ENGLISH SYMPHONY

SYMPHONY SUCCESS

B.B.C. CONCERT OVATION FOR YOUNG COMPOSER

HISTORIC NIGHT FOR BRITISH MUSIC

William Walton's "Compleat Symphony"

COMPOSER'S TRIUMPH

AUDIENCE APPLAUD HIS FIRST SYMPHONY

"Yodelling Song" from the first ballet inspired by *Façade*. It was given at the Chamber Ballet Dancing Theatre in Hagen, Germany on 22 September 1929. The choreography was by Günter Hess and consisted of six "Scenes".

Frederick Ashton choreographed his justly famous version of *Façade* for the Camargo Society's 1931 season at the Cambridge Theatre, London. Lydia Lopokova and Alicia Markova led the company, which included Anthony Tudor and Yehudi Menuhin's future wife, Diana Gould.

"Foxtrot". When the Vic-Wells Ballet Company presented the ballet in 1935, "Country Dance" was added to the existing seven divertissements. Two more numbers: "Noche Espagnole" and "Foxtrot" were added in 1940. The dancers are (left to right): Robert Helpmann, June Brae, Frederick Ashton and Pamela May.

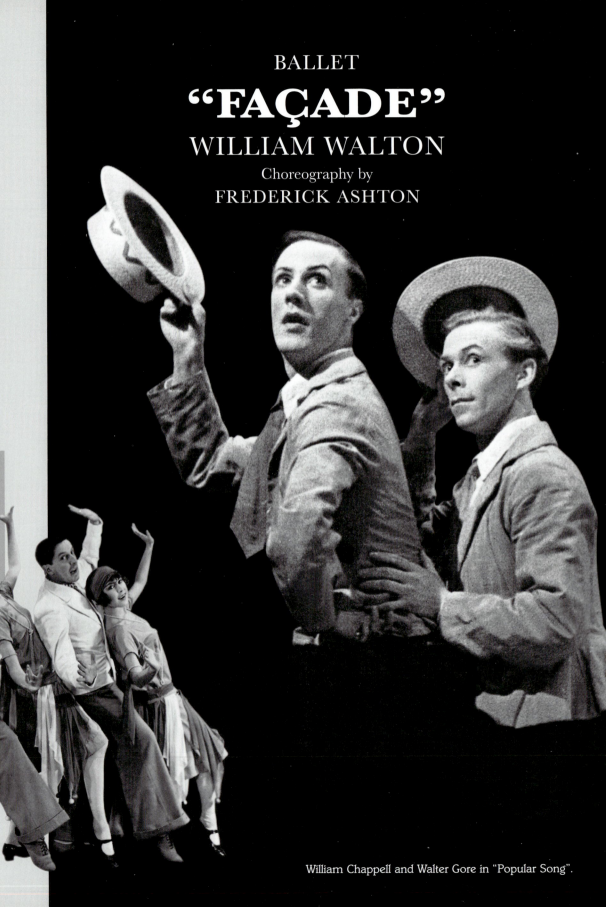

BALLET
"FAÇADE"
WILLIAM WALTON
Choreography by
FREDERICK ASHTON

William Chappell and Walter Gore in "Popular Song".

Walton with his friends "Flo" Lambert and "Fred" Ashton. When she first met her future husband, Florence Lambert was a fourteen-year-old housemaid, said to have been the daughter of a Javanese sailor. Walton was godfather to her son Kit, who later managed "The Who" pop group. Constant Lambert's pet name for his wife was "Mouse". Walton was not the only one to be amused when, after her divorce, she went on to marry a man named "Hole".

Left: Constant Lambert and Margot Fonteyn. In the year of *Façade's* première Lambert became Conductor and Music Director of the Vic-Wells (later Sadler's Wells) Ballet. Fonteyn joined the company in 1935 at the age of fifteen and later danced the solo in Walton's "Polka". For eight years, the married Lambert's life was dominated by a deep and passionate affair with Fonteyn, which she was reluctant to acknowledge in public.

Above left: Alicia Markova in the original costume for "Polka". Above right: Paula Hinton as "The Milkmaid".

Below: "The Tarantella Finale" with the entire company in front of John Armstrong's whimsical set.

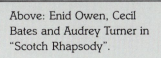

Above: Enid Owen, Cecil Bates and Audrey Turner in "Scotch Rhapsody".

Charles B. COCHRAN'S 1936 REVUE FOLLOW THE SUN

Left: Programme for C.B. Cochran's *1936 Revue*. "Never before has such a riot of colour, glamour and talent been seen on any one stage." (*Sunday Chronicle*) Five years earlier, Walton told Siegfried Sassoon that Cochran was recruiting him "both as a ballet and as a 'jazz' merchant".

Left: Charles B. Cochran (1872–1951) "a very Napoleon of the entertainment industry" (*The Tatler*). He was one of the foremost impresarios of his day. He made and lost several fortunes presenting boxing, wrestling, roller-skating, rodeo and circus as well as his glittering revues.

Below: Scene from *The First Shoot*. This short ballet appeared as Part II Scene 19 of *Follow The Sun*. The scenario (depicting an Edwardian shooting party which goes horribly wrong) was written by Osbert Sitwell; the choreography was by Frederick Ashton with the help of Cecil Beaton, who also designed the costumes. Walton did not know that the pit orchestra included horns until he got to the rehearsal. Parts were added overnight.

Claire Luce, the American actress and dancer, who played Lady de Fontenoy in *The First Shoot*.

HIS MAJESTY'S
THEATRE - - - HAYMARKET, S.W.I
Proprietor : JOSEPH BENSON   Lessees : H. M. & S. LTD.
LICENSED BY THE LORD CHAMBERLAIN TO .. .. .. THOMAS H. BOSTOCK

MONDAY, 14th DECEMBER, 1936, at 8 p.m.
Subsequently :
EVERY EVENING at 8.30
Matinees : Wednesday and Saturday at 2.30
First Matinee : WEDNESDAY, 16th DECEMBER

CHARLES B. COCHRAN
presents
ELISABETH BERGNER
IN
"THE BOY DAVID"
by
J. M. BARRIE

Scenery and Costumes by AUGUSTUS JOHN and ERNST STERN
Music by WILLIAM WALTON
The play directed by KOMISARJEVSKY

SMOKING IS NOT PERMITTED IN THE AUDITORIUM

The Viennese actress Elisabeth
Bergner as *The Boy David*,
a play by the author of *Peter Pan*,
J.M. Barrie.

The programme for *The Boy David*. The play was not a
success; C.B. Cochran, its producer, described it as "the
greatest disappointment of my life". It ran for only seven
weeks. Cochran said: "Never try to reprieve a play when the
best of all critics – the box office – tells you it won't do."

Walton with Elisabeth Bergner and Augustus John
(who designed the sets) taking a bow on the first night
of *The Boy David*. Walton wrote music introducing
each of the play's six scenes.

Far left: *Escape Me Never* (1935).
Bergner starred with Griffith Jones and
Hugh Sinclair. Walton composed the
score while he was trying to work out
how to finish his First Symphony.

Centre left: *A Stolen Life* (1939),
co-starring Michael Redgrave.
The score was recorded by the BBC
Television Orchestra conducted by
Hyam Greenbaum.

Left: *As You Like It* (1936).
The cast included Laurence Olivier
(1907–1989), who played Orlando.

Bottom left: *Dreaming Lips* (1937).
Raymond Massey co-starred with
Bergner. Boyd Neel conducted
Walton's score, which incorporated
sections of the Violin Concertos by
Beethoven and Tchaikovsky played by
Antonio Brosa. Brosa helped Walton
with technical aspects of the Violin
Concerto which he was composing for
Heifetz.

Bergner was married to the film
producer Paul Czinner, who
hired Walton to write the scores
for many of the films he
produced as showcases for his
wife's dazzling talent during the
late 1930s.

79

WILLIAM WALTON'S LATEST TRIUMPH

Composes Coronation March to be Played in the Abbey

THE Oldham-born composer, Mr. William T. Walton, is again in the news. He has been invited to compose the Coronation march, which, it is understood, will be played in Westminster Abbey during the Coronation ceremony on May 12. The work has recently been completed, and is now being scored for a full orchestra. It will shortly be published in this form by the Oxford University Press.

Oldham Chronicle, 5 April 1937.

Walton with his score for the *Coronation March*.
An illustration from *Radio Times*.

An internal BBC memorandum earlier noted that Walton "would love to be commissioned by the corporation to write a really fine symphonic Coronation march. No one will doubt that his immense technical ability should produce a march of equal value to the existing Elgar marches . . . he feels that some sort of immediate financial encouragement would be justified in order to enable him to put some of his work on one side." He was paid 40 guineas.

Lady Wimborne in ceremonial garb. The Coronation of King George VI took place on 12 May 1937.

The Coronation – inside Westminster Abbey. Walton's *Crown Imperial* was performed by The Coronation Orchestra conducted by Adrian Boult during the entrance of George V's widow, Queen Mary, just before the ceremony began. It had been broadcast three days earlier and recorded for HMV the previous month. The words "Crown Imperial" can be found both in Shakespeare's *Henry V* and William Dunbar's *In Honour of the City of London*. Walton's large-scale setting of the Dunbar poem, for chorus and orchestra, came out in December 1937.

The Royal Family on the balcony of Buckingham Palace after the Coronation. To judge from his glum expression, not even Walton's stirring march could reconcile the unhappy monarch to the weight of the crown or the burden of his high office.

Villa Cimbrone, Ravello, Italy. Greta Garbo and her lover Leopold Stokowski had only recently departed when Alice Wimborne rented an apartment here in January 1938 and brought Walton out to convalesce after a hernia operation. Much of his Violin Concerto was composed here.

The Belvedere overlooking the Bay of Naples at Villa Cimbrone. Having been bitten by a tarantula spider, Walton likened the second movement of his Violin Concerto to a tarantella; it has the tempo direction "Presto capriccioso alla napoletana". The trio section, a Canzonetta, resembles a Neapolitan folksong.

Alice Wimborne was the inspiration behind the Violin Concerto which Walton began writing for Jascha Heifetz in 1936.

Jascha Heifetz (1901–1987) was a year older than Walton. Born in Russia, he had settled in the USA and was pre-eminent among the violinists of his generation. He commissioned other concertos from Korngold and Castelnuovo-Tedesco. In May 1939 Walton sailed to New York with Alice on the *SS Normandie* to go over the score with Heifetz: he was afraid it lacked bravura although it is technically very demanding. When they met in Connecticut, Heifetz was more interested in discussing his garden. According to Walton, "as I was leaving the question of being paid arose. Was it £300 or $1,500? I said £300, not realising by then that the pound was a bit shakey even in those days. So he took out a bit of paper, rang up his bank and gave me $1,493 and some cents! He'd made on the deal!"

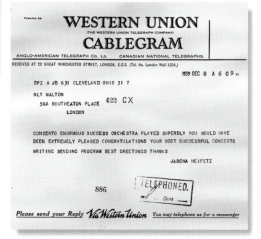

Telegrams about the Violin Concerto from Heifetz, who gave the first performance in Cleveland, Ohio on 7 December 1939. The first British performance was given at the Royal Albert Hall two years later by Henry Holst. Heifetz's annotated copy of the solo part went down with a ship torpedoed in the Atlantic. Luckily a photostat copy had been made. The war prevented Heifetz playing the work in Britain until 1950.

Spike Hughes (1908–1987), writer, broadcaster and jazz bassist. In his autobiography *Opening Bars* he tells of introducing Walton to Heifetz at the Berkeley Hotel. They lunched on smoked salmon and tournedos. Walton was godfather to one of Hughes's daughters.

"I seriously advise all sensitive composers to die at the age of 37. I know! I have gone through the first halcyon periods and am just about ripe for critical damnation."

Walton to an American interviewer in 1939.

Musical Evening at Wimborne House by Sir John Lavery. Lord Wimborne can be seen bottom left; Walton reclines on the sofa next to him; Alice Wimborne is seated extreme right, next to her is Garrett Moore, later Lord Drogheda, who became Chairman of the Royal Opera House, Covent Garden. Walton arranged for music by Benjamin Britten to be played at another of these soirées.

CHAPTER 5

PUBLIC SERVICE & PRIVATE GRIEF
1939–1948

"The War actually divided my life into two halves." WALTON

THE WAR YEARS were desperately frustrating for a man whose inner life depended upon creativity. The slow but steady flow of major compositions that had characterised the previous decade came to a halt, to be replaced by ephemeral work for stage, radio and cinema.

At the outbreak of the war Walton enrolled as an ambulance driver for the local Air Raid Precautions centre near Alice Wimborne's country home outside Rugby. Work on anything with intellectual pretensions seemed impossible but he wrote a set of ten short piano *Duets for Children* (dedicated to his niece and nephew) and early in 1940 orchestrated some cantata movements by J.S. Bach, among them "Sheep may safely graze", for Frederick Ashton to choreograph for an abstract ballet entitled *The Wise Virgins*. The score was dedicated to the wisest virgin he knew, Edith Sitwell. A film score followed, for G.B. Shaw's *Major Barbara,* directed by Gabriel Pascal and starring Wendy Hiller and Rex Harrison. But between the Violin Concerto of 1939 and the second string quartet of 1947 Walton composed few works of any substance: the brilliant *Scapino* overture (a commission from the Chicago Symphony Orchestra), a 45-minute ballet, *The Quest*, written in haste for the Sadler's Wells company, and a fine setting of a John Masefield poem for unaccompanied chorus, *Where Does the Uttered Music Go?* which was sung at the unveiling of a memorial window for Sir Henry Wood in 1946.

In 1941 Walton was called up, only to be exempted from military service in order to compose music for films deemed to be of national importance. The first of these was *Next of Kin,* for which he dashed off thirty minutes of music in three weeks, with the assistance of a devoted young musician, Roy Douglas, who worked on the orchestration. Only days later he started on twenty minutes of incidental music for a stage production of *Macbeth,* starring John Gielgud; it was all composed in the week between Christmas and

New Year's Day, 1942. Walton was living permanently at Lady Wimborne's, Lord Wimborne having died in 1939; his own little house in Belgravia had been destroyed by a German bomb the previous May, in the same air raid that flattened the Queen's Hall. In 1942 Walton was made civilian adviser to the Army Film Unit. The job was to propose composers for specific film projects. It was, he wrote, "my first experience of a government department; it stank of red tape, but I found everyone very nice." About his own work he had no illusions. He was commissioned to compose music for a substantial BBC radio feature, *Christopher Columbus*, in which Laurence Olivier was to play the hero: "I can't treat C.C in any way different from a rather superior film", Walton wrote to his enthusiastic supporter, the radio and film producer Dallas Bower: "the music is entirely occasional and is of no use other than what it is meant for." (He was soon to rethink this unduly modest assessment.) His subsequent wartime films included *The Foreman Went to France*, with the comedian Tommy Trinder, *Went the Day Well?* (from a Graham Greene short story) and *The First of the Few*, starring Leslie Howard, from which he extracted a popular concert-hall work entitled *Prelude and Fugue (The "Spitfire")*. In 1944 came *Henry V*, the first and most powerful of the three Shakespeare films he scored for Laurence Olivier; it gave an enormous boost to public morale in the last year of the war and is one of the masterpieces of cinematic art.

But when peace came it brought with it, for Walton, a sense of failure. His position as the country's leading composer was increasingly challenged by Benjamin Britten, eleven years his junior. Walton had recognised his genius early on (they first met in 1937) and spoke on his behalf when Britten had to appear at a tribunal examining conscientious objectors after his return from the USA in 1942. But while Walton was doing his bit for the war effort and developing a new persona as an Establishment power-broking figure, agreeing to serve on various committees and councils and even putting his name to an impressive blueprint for a future national opera company at Covent Garden, Britten had been composing a string of masterpieces, culminating in his enormously impressive opera *Peter Grimes,* which was mounted at Sadler's Wells in June 1945 only a month after the war in Europe ended. Privately Walton jokingly labelled it "Grimy Pete" but writing to the composer he praised it unstintingly as "a quite extraordinary achievement". Just as the success of the younger Constant Lambert's *Rio Grande* in 1929 had stimulated the composition of *Belshazzar's Feast* so now Walton resolved to write his own opera in response to *Grimes.* But he hesitated before taking the plunge. He made no bones about envying Britten his compositional facility and admitted to Roy Douglas that he had been involved too long in film music. Already in 1939 he had told Dora Foss, the wife of his publisher, that after the Violin Concerto he intended "to learn composition and start in chamber music". Since January 1945 he had been mulling over a string quartet: "I'm in a suicidal struggle with four strings", he told Douglas; "brick walls, slit trenches, Siegfried Lines bristle as never before!" Two months later: "I've captured a trench and overcome some barbed wire entanglements – but every bar is a pill box."

The quartet was eventually premièred two years later, in May 1947, on the BBC's new Third Programme. One of the most perceptive music critics, Desmond Shawe Taylor, wrote that he enjoyed its "blend of harmonic astringency, rhythmic and contrapuntal ingenuity, and nostalgic meditation". Despite the passage of time, Walton's music was, he wrote – and this was a lethal phrase, however kindly intended – "in all the essentials the mixture as before". A younger critic, Michael Kennedy, was later to detect in the quartet a new mood: "the haunting self-communing that is in most of Walton's music is here of a deeper cast, less Angst-ridden but no less deeply felt". At the time, however, there was a discernible feeling among the intelligentsia that Walton's time was passing.

By 1947 he felt ready for the challenge of an opera. Both his muse Alice Wimborne and the BBC, which offered him a commission, encouraged his endeavours. A subject was chosen, the tale of Troilus and his faithless Cressida, as told by Chaucer rather than Shakespeare. A librettist was found in the poet Christopher Hassall, who had learnt his theatrical trade writing the books and lyrics for a string of Ivor Novello musicals. But still Walton could not or would not give the project his undivided attention. Olivier offered him a new film, *Hamlet.* Impossible to refuse! Then Alice fell ill while in Switzerland, en route for a Capri holiday. They desperately needed cash to pay her hospital bills (currency restrictions were stringent) and a chance meeting with Yehudi Menuhin's future wife Diana on a Swiss train led to an unexpected commission for another chamber work, a sonata for violin and piano.

Sadly Alice Wimborne's illness, cancer of the bronchus, did not respond to treatment. Walton worked feverishly on *Hamlet* during her long illness that winter – an hour of music was needed – and then watched her die, in great pain, before he could commence the opera project upon which she had set such great store. She had warned the librettist that although her man was a chronic procrastinator, "one day the ball will bounce against an electric wire as was the case with *Belshazzar".* But before he had composed a note of *Troilus* Walton's life was to undergo seismic changes. Recovering from jaundice and anxious to shake off his depression in the wake of Alice's death, he took a holiday on Capri with his painter friend Michael Ayrton. He found some solace with a young Swedish painter, Ann Bergson, and there was even talk of an engagement – but Walton had already agreed to represent British composers in a delegation visiting South America and when he returned from Buenos Aires in January 1949 it was not a Swedish but an Argentinian bride he presented to his astonished friends.

Wartime poster for National Service. "The problem was, what could I usefully do?" Walton had been too young to fight in the First World War and was now at 37 too old for immediate recruitment in the Second. He continued to compose.

Walton enrolled as an ambulance driver for the local ARP (Air Raid Precautions). "I was taught to drive this very heavy vehicle but after I'd run it into a ditch several times, they said perhaps you'd better *not* drive an ambulance."

WILLIAM WALTON'S NEW CONCERTO:

Ambulance Work Keeps Him From Premiere

AMBULANCE work in England prevented Mr. William Walton, of Oldham, the well-known composer, from being present at the premiere of his new violin concerto when it was performed by Jascha Heifetz and the Cleveland Orchestra, wires Reuter from Cleveland, Ohio. He cables that he was driving an ambulance in London and was awaiting orders to go to France.

The composer dedicated the concerto to Heifetz, whom he authorised to make such changes in the composition as he might consider necessary.

Mr. Arthur Rodiznski, conductor of the orchestra, said that the concerto was "absolutely one of the finest violin concertos ever written."

Oldham newspaper report, 8 December 1939.

Fire fighting during the London Blitz. "I had just bought a house in Belgravia and it got bombed flat."

Major Barbara (1941). A starry cast was headed by Wendy Hiller and Rex Harrison. George Bernard Shaw adapted his play for the screen. Walton was fascinated by the writer's dentures. "Every time he opened his mouth, his dental plate came down and then went up – very off-putting."

Walton was eventually called up in 1941 but was exempted from military service on condition that he wrote music for films supporting the war effort. No less than four films came out in 1942. First to be composed was

"The Next Of Kin" (January 1942). The cast included Jack Hawkins and Thora Hird. Walton himself appeared as an extra, dressed as an officer.

"The Foreman Went To France" (April 1942). The narrative was by J.B. Priestley, based on a true story; the film featured Tommy Trinder and Gordon Jackson as two soldiers helping to rescue vital machinery from the hands of the invading Germans.

"The First Of The Few" (August 1942). A dramatised biography of R. J. Mitchell (played by Leslie Howard), the designer of the Spitfire fighter plane. The score was composed when the war news was at its gloomiest. The March and Fugue were soon re-scored and often played as concert music.

"Went The Day Well?" (November 1942). Graham Greene wrote this thriller about fifth columnists in wartime England. The film featured Thora Hird as a flighty seductress.

Ashby St Ledgers, Alice Wimborne's 14th century country home near Rugby. Walton retreated there to compose during the war. His colleague Roy Douglas remembers that "after dinner William would often go away and write some film music and then bring it to play to Lady W. and myself and I have known her to say: 'that's not really good enough, William, you can write a better tune than that.' And he would immediately go back to the music room and do so." During the war Alice liked to smoke cigars presented to her by her relative, Winston Churchill.

SCAPINO

A Comedy Overture

WILLIAM WALTON

OXFORD UNIVERSITY PRESS

The score of *Scapino*, A Comedy Overture, inspired by an etching by Jacques Callot. It was commissioned by the Chicago Symphony Orchestra to celebrate its 50th birthday, the first of many American orchestral commissions.

"Better be with the dead than on the torture of the mind to lie in restless ecstasy". John Gielgud and Gwen Ffrangcon-Davies as Macbeth and Lady Macbeth.

A wartime photo of Walton at the rostrum. Despite his effective technique and his inspirational quality, Walton always restricted his conducting to his own music.

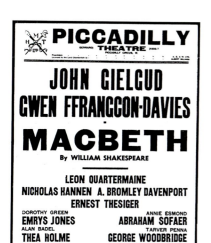

PICCADILLY THEATRE

JOHN GIELGUD
GWEN FFRANGCON-DAVIES
·
MACBETH
By WILLIAM SHAKESPEARE
──────────
LEON QUARTERMAINE
NICHOLAS HANNEN   A. BROMLEY DAVENPORT
ERNEST THESIGER
DOROTHY GREEN   ANNIE ESMOND
EMRYS JONES   **ABRAHAM SOFAER**
ALAN BADEL   TARVER PENNA
THEA HOLME   **GEORGE WOODBRIDGE**
FRANCES RUTTLEDGE   CHARLES MAUNSELL
FRANCIS LISTER
──────────
JOHN GIELGUD'S PRODUCTION
Decor by MICHAEL AYRTON and JOHN MINTON
Incidental Music by WILLIAM WALTON   Fights and Movements by SURIA MAGITO

Above: Walton wrote a substantial score for Gielgud's 1942 production of the Scottish Play. Gielgud reported that after he had attended rehearsals Walton "decided to compose background music for the scenes of the witches in accordance with the rhythms of their verses . . . I gave him the timings for the interludes and some scene changes and was amazed to find he had observed them meticulously".

Below: Walton was always a keen radio listener. His fruitful relationship with the BBC took another step forward when he composed the music for Dallas Bower's 1942 radio production of *Christopher Columbus* by Louis MacNeice. The broadcast commemorated the 450th anniversary of the discovery of the Americas. The USA had just entered the war.

Above: A studio rehearsal for *Christopher Columbus*.
The producer Dallas Bower (in shirt-sleeves and wearing glasses) is in the middle, with the poet Louis MacNeice next to him, right.

Laurence Olivier played the role of Columbus. He was an officer in the Fleet Air Arm at the time.

Left: November 1941, the BBC Symphony Orchestra rehearsing Walton's Violin Concerto with Henry Holst as soloist in its wartime base, the Bedford Corn Exchange, under the bâton of the composer. The British première of *Scapino* was included in the same programme, which was broadcast live to the nation.

Wartime Ballets with Frederick Ashton

The Quest - Scene 1: "Outside The House Of Archimago" (Robert Helpmann as St George; Margot Fonteyn as Una; Alexis Rassine as Sansloy).

The Wise Virgins

Music by J. S. Bach.   Orchestrated by William Walton.

Décor and Costumes by Rex Whistler.

Choreography by Frederick Ashton.

The Bridegroom .... MICHAEL SOMES

The Bride .... MARGOT FONTEYN

The Father .... CLAUDE NEWMAN

Her Mother .... ANNABEL FARJEON

Wise Virgins ... JULIA FARRON, OLIVE DEACON, JOAN LEAMAN, JOAN PHILLIPS, PALMA NYE

Foolish Virgins ... MARY HONER, ELIZABETH KENNEDY, JOY NEWTON, PATRICIA GARNETT, JEAN BEDELLS

Angels ... RICHARD ELLIS, JOHN HART, LESLIE EDWARDS, LEO YOUNG, STANLEY HALL

Cherubs ... DERYK MENDEL, MARGARET DALE, GUINEVERE PARRY, MAVIS JACKSON

INTERVAL

Michael Somes and Margot Fonteyn in the 1940 ballet *The Wise Virgins*, choreographed at Sadler's Wells by Frederick Ashton; the décor and costumes were designed by Rex Whistler. The music, by J.S. Bach, was chosen by Constant Lambert and orchestrated by Walton. Fonteyn was amused to see the ballet advertised on a bill-board as "*The Wise Virgins* – subject to alteration".

The Quest - Scene 3: "The Palace Of Pride" (Moira Shearer as Pride surrounded by Courtiers). Moira Shearer made her professional debut in *The Quest*. She was only seventeen and a strikingly beautiful red-head. She went on to star in *The Red Shoes*. Sacheverell Sitwell was later to harbour an unrequited passion for her.

Right: Playbill for *The Quest*, a ballet in five scenes based on Edmund Spenser's *Faerie Queene* with choreography by Ashton and sets by John Piper. It was intended as a patriotic gesture, evoking a mythical England. The collaboration was difficult; Ashton only had five weeks' leave from the Royal Air Force and would have liked to immerse himself in a completed score, but Walton wrote the numbers piecemeal on the backs of envelopes and would "bribe guards on trains to take a minute or so's music to wherever Freddie happened to be with the ballet company – to Wolverhampton, Preston or somewhere".

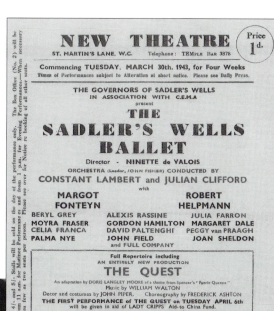

Below: *The Quest* - Scene 5: "The House Of Holiness" After pledging himself to England, St George (Robert Helpmann) bids farewell to his beloved Una (Margot Fonteyn) and departs on his Quest, waved off by attendant Virtues. Ashton's biographer suggested caustically that the Virtues resembled G.I. brides waving goodbye to their loved ones. "Bobby Helpmann looked more like the Dragon than St. George", the composer remembered. Walton spoke fondly of the music he wrote to depict the Seven Deadly Sins: a Passacaglia "could have been magnificent if there had been any orchestra".

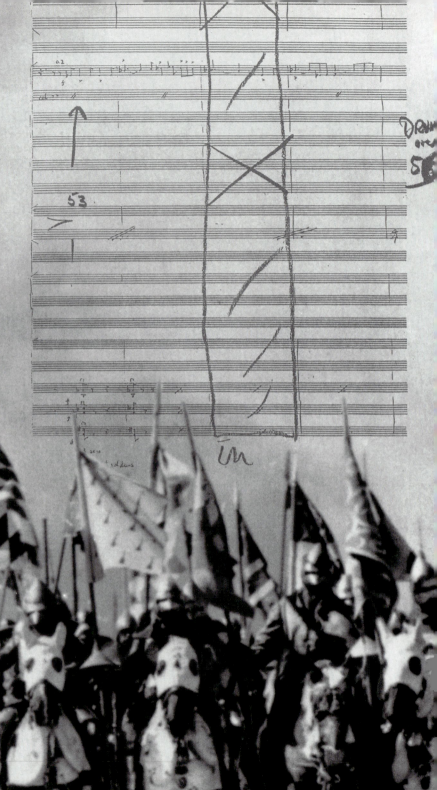

Henry V film poster, 1944. Some of the most memorable sections of the score, including "The Death of Falstaff" were composed before Walton saw the film footage; once again he was responding to text as he had done in *Façade* and *Belshazzar's Feast*.

"Charge and Battle". Walton incorporated the melody of a fifteenth-century French battle-song, suggested to him by Vaughan Williams.

"Cry God for Harry, England and St George"

Laurence Olivier as Henry V. Olivier described Walton's score as "the most wonderful I've ever heard for a film. In fact for me the music actually makes the film."

Part of Walton's manuscript for the opening of the Battle Charge. His handwritten notes at the bottom indicate "French foot soldiers", "Drums in faster rhythm"(4/4), "French Cavalry" and "Standards lowered".

In 1942 Walton was awarded an Honorary Doctorate of Music by Oxford University.

Oxford Degree Ceremony. Malcolm Sargent (right) received a degree in the same ceremony. "Flash Harry" as he was later known by generations of Promenaders, was seven years older than Walton and at the time conductor of the Hallé Orchestra.

The Royal Opera House, Covent Garden. In the spring of 1944 Walton injured his eye and was forced to dictate to Alice Wimborne the text of a report he was working on concerning the future of British opera at Covent Garden.

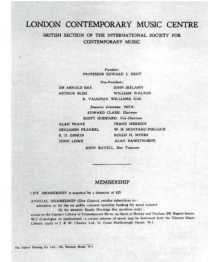

The composer Alan Rawsthorne (1905–1971). With the painter Michael Ayrton (1920–1975), he formed part of the drinking circle whose company Walton enjoyed on his visits to London. One of their favourite haunts, The George, near Broadcasting House was nicknamed "The Gluepot" because so many musicians got stuck inside it. Walton served with Rawsthorne on the board of the London Contemporary Music Centre.

Letter to Edward Dent (6 October 1941). Walton was campaigning to keep the eccentric John Christie, founder of Glyndebourne Opera, from taking control of Covent Garden.

Sir Henry Wood, the founder and conductor of the Promenade Concerts, died in 1944. In his memory Walton composed *Where Does the Uttered Music Go?* to a poem by John Masefield. It was first sung at the unveiling of a memorial window at the Church of St Sepulchure, High Holborn, London, where Henry Wood had played the organ as a boy. Scenes from his life are depicted in the lower panels: the central figure is that of St Cecilia, patron saint of music.

Benjamin Britten (1913–1976). Walton befriended him in 1937. Britten, then 23, noted in his diary: "he is so obviously the head-prefect of English music, whereas I'm the promising new boy." Britten had produced a string of masterpieces since his return to England from the USA in 1942 and with *Peter Grimes*, first seen in 1945, he eclipsed the older man.

Sadler's Wells programme for the Spring 1945 season.

SADLER'S WELLS

ROSEBERY AVENUE, E.C.1   BOX OFFICE : TER. 1672
LICENSEE : TYRONE GUTHRIE   MANAGER : GERALD SEYMOUR

THE GOVERNORS OF SADLER'S WELLS
IN ASSOCIATION WITH C.E.M.A.
PRESENT

SADLER'S WELLS OPERA

MADAM BUTTERFLY   LA BOHEME
THE BARTERED BRIDE   COSI FAN TUTTE
RIGOLETTO
AND FIRST PRODUCTION OF
PETER GRIMES
BY BENJAMIN BRITTEN

ADMINISTRATORS OF THE OLD VIC AND SADLER'S WELLS COMPANIES
TYRONE GUTHRIE

Cast list for *Peter Grimes*. Britten fell out with Sadler's Wells and took his next venture, the opera *The Rape of Lucretia*, to Glyndebourne.

THURSDAY EVE., JUNE 7TH   SATURDAY EVE., JUNE 9TH

PETER GRIMES

An Opera by BENJAMIN BRITTEN
Libretto by MONTAGU SLATER, based on the poem of George Crabbe
Conductor—REGINALD GOODALL

Peter Grimes (a Fisherman)	PETER PEARS
Ellen Orford (the Borough Schoolmistress)	JOAN CROSS
Auntie (Landlady of "The Boar")	EDITH COATES
Her "Nieces"	BLANCHE TURNER, MINNIA BOWER
Balstrode (a retired Sea-Captain)	RODERICK JONES
Mrs. Sedley (a Widow)	VALETTA IACOPI
Swallow (Lawyer and Magistrate)	OWEN BRANNIGAN
Ned Keene (Apothecary)	EDMUND DONLEVY
Bob Boles (a Methodist Fisherman)	MORGAN JONES
The Rector	TOM CULBERT
Hobson (The Village Carrier)	FRANK VAUGHAN
Doctor Thorp	SASA MACHOV
A Boy (Grimes' new apprentice)	LEONARD THOMPSON

The People of the Borough : Maude Boughton, Muriel Burnett, Peggy Butler, Rose Carlton, Myfanwy Edwards, Pauline Guy, Hilda Hanson, Netta Leggat, Jean Mountford, Winifred Newnham, Olwen Price, Keturah Sorrell, Molly Wilkinson ; Howard Allport, Gilbert Bailey, William Benn, William Booth, Albert Digney, George Gorst, Eldon Guller, Leonard Hanks, John Havard, Leonard Hodgkinson, Ivor Ingham, Cecil Lloyd, Haydn Meredith, Charles Miller, Arthur Perrow, Erin Tosi, Herbert Tree, Rhys Williams, Vaughan Williams ; Margaret Aspin, Romayne Austin, Barbara Fewster, Fiona Moore

Peter Pears (1910–1986) as Peter Grimes in the title role of the 1945 production. Later he sang a major role in Walton's opera *Troilus and Cressida* and became an outstanding reciter of *Façade*.

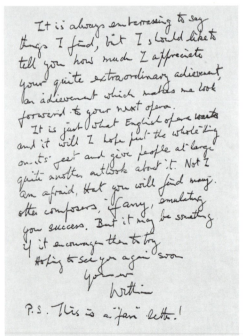

Walton's "fan" letter to Britten, June 1945. After attending the première of *Peter Grimes*, Walton wrote enthusiastically: "It is just what English opera wants."

A recording session for *Hamlet* with the recently-formed Philharmonia Orchestra. John Hollingsworth conducted

Poster for *Hamlet*, 1948. The film was made in black and white after Olivier fell out with the Technicolor company.

A J·ARTHUR RANK ENTERPRISE

Laurence Olivier
presents

HAMLET
by William Shakespeare

A TWO CITIES FILM
under the management of
FILIPPO DEL GIUDICE

DISTRIBUTION by EAGLE LION

Walton, with Muir Mathieson (1911–1975) (left) and Laurence Olivier (right). Mathieson was to have conducted the sessions himself, but had broken his right arm falling off his horse. He was an important figure in British films, having commissioned Arthur Bliss to compose *Things to Come* in 1935 and Ralph Vaughan Williams for *49th Parallel* in 1941. In 1946 he directed the original film of Britten's *Young Person's Guide to the Orchestra*.

A post-war portrait of Walton, pipe in hand, by Bill Brandt. Giacomo Rossini (on the wall), famed for his wit, had been a favourite of Walton's ever since he parodied *William Tell* in his *Façade*. Walton was in search of an operatic subject: he had mentioned his ambition to compose for the operatic stage as early as 1934.

The Blech Quartet. They gave the first performance of Walton's Second String Quartet in 1947. Left to right: Keith Cummings (viola); Lionel Bentley and Harry Blech (violins) and Douglas Cameron (cello). Walton was happy to return to abstract music after a decade hitherto immersed in work for cinema, stage and radio.

Christopher Hassall. (1912–1963), actor, playwright, poet and lyricist. He wrote the books for seven of Ivor Novello's musical shows. He and Walton began work on *Troilus and Cressida* in 1947.

Alice Wimborne. After her husband's death in 1939 she had hoped to marry Walton. She thought of *Troilus and Cressida* as "our child". She told Hassall not to be worried by Walton's apparent procrastination.

Lowndes Cottage, bequeathed to Walton by Lady Wimborne.

Letter from Alice Wimborne to Christopher Hassall, 15 June 1947. Alice understood Walton's creative process. She was "very good at making me work" Walton said.

The Times, 25 June 1948. Alice had died of cancer on April 19, 1948. Her last hours were agonisingly painful. Walton never forgot how she had turned black through lack of oxygen.

A legacy of £10,000, her leasehold residence, Lowndes Cottage, motor-car and certain effects were left by the Dowager Viscountess Wimborne to William Walton, the Oldham-born, composer.

The Dowager Viscountess, whose will is published today, left £100,468 gross (duty paid £44,557). She was one of the best-known political hostesses of her time.

"It was all very, very sad …
One forgets about it if one can."

Portrait of Alice Wimborne by Sir John Lavery.

Portrait sketch of Walton by Michael Ayrton.

CHAPTER 6

MARRIAGE & EXILE

1948–1956

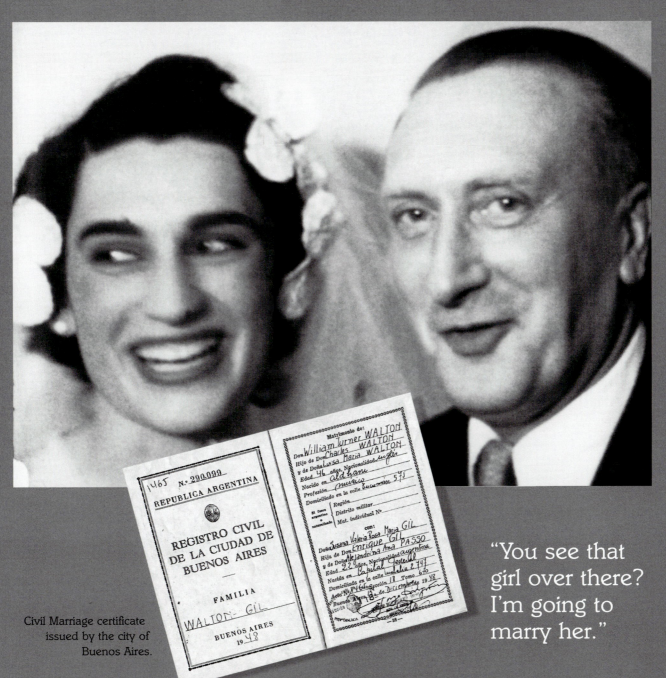

Civil Marriage certificate
issued by the city of
Buenos Aires.

"You see that
girl over there?
I'm going to
marry her."

IN SEPTEMBER 1948 William Walton sailed from Genoa to Buenos Aires, where he joined a high-powered British delegation from the Performing Right Society seeking to persuade the Argentinians to sign the Berne copyright convention. Walton was a staunch supporter of the PRS; he persuaded his reluctant publisher to join the organisation after signing up individually as a composer. Walton had become an establishment figure (he was knighted three years later) although by temperament he was hardly a "meetings man". Nevertheless the conference in South America, preceded by a lengthy sea voyage, must have been a welcome diversion from his personal depression and his writer's block – the two had gone hand in hand for nearly twenty years. An extended spell overseas was also the best way to evade the attentions of Ann Bergson, the young Swedish painter to whom he had rashly proposed marriage the previous summer on the island of Capri.

Michael Ayrton's portrait of the brooding composer (see page 102) reveals how deeply Walton felt the death of Alice Wimborne.

Walton, still a heart-throb in his forties.
"It was the most appalling sort of
wedding – at nine o'clock at night,
in devastating heat."

He must also have been depressed by his sagging post-war reputation. In Buenos Aires the publisher Leslie Boosey was the principal British negotiator; Walton was standing next to him at a press conference when, with mind-boggling tactlessness, he announced to the journalists that Benjamin Britten (whose works Boosey's firm handled) was the UK's leading composer. Happily there was instant compensation for the wounded Walton: he caught the eye of the British Council's social secretary, a vivacious girl of 22: "We met, went off to lunch and I proposed to her the next day. As far as I remember, she said 'Don't be ridiculous, Dr Walton', but we got engaged three weeks after that".

Susana Gil Passo was the daughter of a prominent lawyer who also owned a substantial cattle ranch. She had had an unconventional education, spoke fluent English and had already accompanied her father on a lecture tour in the United States before she joined the British Council's Argentina office as a press secretary. The sceptical Señor Gil urged caution, pointing out the difference in ages – Susana was 24 years younger than Walton. (Incidentally, the recently deceased Alice Wimborne had been 22 years his senior!) But Susana was a determined woman and the impetuous William held his ground. His proposal had been an uncharacteristically bold gesture for a man who had once spent seven months contemplating a single recalcitrant musical phrase. To marry somebody outside his social world who had little knowledge of classical music, let alone of the British arts world with which he had been so intimately connected for 25 years, suggests that he had decided, come what may, to change once again the course of his life. As a boy his parents had helped him to escape from Oldham; the Sitwells led him away from the potentially dead hand of academia when he was an Oxford undergraduate, and in the mid-1930s his affair with Alice Wimborne gave him freedom from financial worries and a measure of emotional security. Now the *coup de foudre* with Susana seems to have prompted him to turn his back on England. Their love at first sight was not to be thwarted by Señor Gil and before the year was out they were married in a civil ceremony, followed five weeks later, in January 1949, by a splendid church wedding attended by four ambassadors and two thousand guests. But the path of true love did not always run smoothly: on the voyage back to England Walton broke the news to his virgin bride that he did not want children. In her memoirs, published after his death, Susana Walton revealed that when later she became pregnant he obliged her to have an abortion.

In gloomy post-war London the Waltons made a dashing entrance on the artistic scene. They set up home in Lowndes Cottage, the Belgravia house that Alice had bequeathed to Walton along with her Bentley and £10,000. The art historian Sir Kenneth Clark and his wife Jane gave a welcoming party. Christabel Aberconway confided to Susana that of all the women in the room she was probably the only one with whom Walton had not slept in his younger days. Walton always had a roving eye but Christabel was no doubt referring in particular to Jane Clark, with whom Walton had had an affair while Alice was still alive. Mrs Walton's own parties were eagerly anticipated in those meat-rationed and gastronomically-impoverished times: her trousseau included two hams and a sack of sugar and every week she received a consignment of five kilos of the best Argentinian beef, forwarded from Buenos Aires in the diplomatic bag.

The long estrangement from the Sitwells ended after Lady Wimborne's death and Walton's subsequent marriage. A fresh Sitwellian collaboration, for Walton's proposed new opera, might have been on the cards. It was the Sitwells' verbal magic, after all, that had sparked off his creativity for *Façade* and *Belshazzar's Feast* in the 1920s. But the choice of Christopher Hassall as his librettist had been pushed through by Alice Wimborne, Hassall's

principal supporter, while she was still alive and Walton was faithful to her memory.

Walton made a brief visit to Oldham to introduce his mother to his South American bride. "Has the Pope got him?", she asked Noel, William's elder brother. Then before embarking on the long haul of an opera he cleared the decks by completing the Sonata for Violin and Piano commissioned from him by Yehudi Menuhin in 1947; it was dedicated to Menuhin's second wife Diana and her sister Griselda, with whom Walton was always very close. The sonata's 1950 London première was later described by Walton himself, in characteristically deflationary style, as a flop; the work was very good, he said, but his idiom was out of date. Walton's biographer, Michael Kennedy, disagreed, hailing the sonata as one of its creator's greatest works "by reason of its sustained inventiveness and mastery of the violin's expressive capacity." Kennedy added that it reflects the tensions felt by Walton in the period of Alice's illness and death.

Señorita Susana Gil Passo in 1944,
four years before her marriage
to Dr Walton.

Walton was not in London for the first performance. During their honeymoon voyage to England he had sprung another surprise on Susana: they were going to live in Italy. Lowndes Cottage would be let to tenants (the first were Laurence Olivier and Vivien Leigh) and he would work on the new opera in the Mediterranean sunshine. The Waltons left London for good in the autumn of 1949, setting up home not, as one might have expected, in Ravello or his beloved Amalfi, where he had spent many months in the 1920s with the Sitwell brothers, but on the relatively unfashionable island of Ischia in the Bay of Naples. Less blatantly romantic than its neighbour Capri, Ischia had been renowned since Roman times for its defunct volcano, Mount Epomeo, and for the bubbling hot springs and healing mud baths that spring from its lava-rich earth. Ischia had no piped water and few roads when the Waltons arrived but the climate was benign, the wine most agreeable and the postal service intermittently adequate – an important consideration during the lengthy composition of the opera *Troilus and Cressida*. From his new home in an abandoned convent, San Francesco, not far from the bustling little town of Forio d'Ischia, Walton was to dispatch dozens of fascinating work-letters to his London-based librettist.

In his Chelsea days Walton had been a gregarious soul but as his music deepened in its expressive power so he came to prefer long periods of compositional solitude. He was to live on Ischia in voluntary exile for the final 33 years of his life, with *Troilus and Cressida* dominating the first half-decade. For an opera that runs little more than two hours (plus intervals) it can be said to have occupied an excessively long period of Walton's working life. He started sketching the music in 1949 and five years later, only three months before the Covent Garden première, he was still demanding re-writes to the libretto and tinkering with the music of the final scene. He was surprisingly unsure of himself and proved ultra-sensitive to criticism from friends throughout the *Troilus* years. The

basic problem, never successfully addressed, was the choice of Christopher Hassall as his librettist. Walton wrote that on occasions Hassall's high-falutin poetry evoked "the worst type of music from me – real neo-Novelloisms which I fear cannot be tolerated on the operatic stage." Some of the harshest reactions, unfortunately not documented, apparently came from his friend Walter Legge, the noted recording producer. Walton is said to have had in his mind's ear the voice of Legge's future wife, Elisabeth Schwarzkopf, when he composed the role of Cressida but despite his considerable prestige he failed to get the diva's commitment in advance; it is fair to surmise that Legge advised her to take other engagements so that she could plead non-availability. (The additional excuse that she was not happy singing in English can be ignored since she had premièred the role of Anne Trulove in Stravinsky's *The Rake's Progress* in 1951 and also sang Belinda in the famous Kirsten Flagstad recording of Purcell's *Dido and Aeneas*.)

Other suggestions concerning the structure of the opera, many of them involving substantial re-writes, came from a new friend and neighbour, the Anglo-American poet W.H. Auden, who spent his summers in Ischia with his partner Chester Kallman. They came with the prestige of having supplied Stravinsky with the libretto for *The Rake's Progress*; Auden had also collaborated with Walton's successful young rival Benjamin Britten on the opera *Paul Bunyan* and had written the texts of two of Britten's most impressive vocal works, *Our Hunting Fathers* and the *Hymn to St Cecilia*. Auden offered good advice and even sketched an entire scene in the third act, but for all his skill as a script doctor he could not turn the wimpish Troilus into a flesh and blood character. Cressida – sexy, vulnerable and traitorous – is a much more interesting creation: Walton's fascination with her must surely be linked to his failed love affair with Imma von Doernberg. But only the high-camp role of Pandarus (modelled on the personality of a well-known civil servant, Sir Edward Marsh) was perfectly conceived – and wittily interpreted at the première by Peter Pears.

The production preparations were dogged by bad luck and exacerbated by Walton's procrastination. (It's even been suggested that the Good Life, Italian style, made him lazy.) Cut off from England, he was ill-informed concerning the capability of the resident singers in the Covent Garden company and poorly placed to influence important creative decisions concerning the première. He wanted the set designs to create a monolithic, timeless quality that would emphasise man's insignificance as the playthings of the gods; his exciting first choice as designer was Henry Moore but the sculptor declined, to be replaced by the architect Sir Hugh Casson, who had done the sets for Glyndebourne's *Alceste* the previous year. Walton thought Casson's designs were "elegant but slight". He was even more disappointed when his preferred stage director, Laurence Olivier, had to cancel because of filming commitments, to be replaced by the gifted but operatically inexperienced George Devine. As his Troilus, Walton hoped for the young Swedish tenor Nicolai Gedda but had to make do with the histrionically sedate Richard Lewis. Instead of Schwarzkopf as his Cressida, he accepted his friend Hans Werner Henze's suggestion and opted for the beautiful and intelligent Hungarian soprano Magda Lázslò. Ironically, an Argentinian, Susana Walton, had the tough task of coaching her in English.

The broadcast of the première preserved in the BBC Archive proves how strongly the company had pulled together in the final days of rehearsal despite questionable leadership from Sir Malcolm Sargent. The conductor had not been in Covent Garden's orchestra pit since 1936 and it was clear to impartial observers, among them Jascha Heifetz, that he was not familiar with the score – yet he seemed intent on tampering with it, making changes in the orchestration after every run-through. Critical response to the London production in December 1954 was positive, however, and Walton's international reputation ensured other *Troilus and Cressida* productions over the next two years at San Francisco Opera, the New York City Center and, most significantly, La Scala, Milan. The critic of *Il Tempo* was quite enthusiastic "To Walton's essentially retiring, dry, musical temperament there is added a superimposed rhetorical style, an accent that is truly operatic, and which lies somewhere between Verdi and so-called *verismo*." But *La Patria* recorded that "mingled with the loud applause were hisses and catcalls". Walton sat that night between two Cressidas-that-might-have-been who were appearing in other operas at La Scala, the divas Maria Callas and Elisabeth Schwarzkopf. *Troilus* contains gorgeous, full-blooded passages as sumptuous as any in the works of Puccini, to whose tradition it actually lies closest, but to this day it has never received a performance in which the three principal roles have all been ideally cast.

In 1953 Walton briefly suspended his operatic labours to re-assert himself as Britain's best composer of occasional music since Elgar. For the Coronation of Queen Elizabeth II he produced *Orb and Sceptre,* a ceremonial march to set alongside his 1937 *Crown Imperial.* A more significant addition to the celebratory repertoire was a superlative *Coronation Te Deum* for massive forces: two mixed choirs, two semi-choruses, boys' voices, organ, orchestra and military brass. Even on disc the effect is powerful; in Westminster Abbey it must have been overwhelming. Walton therefore would have seemed the obvious choice to become Master of the Queen's Music in succession to Arnold Bax, who died four months after the Coronation. Instead the post went to Arthur Bliss – presumably because Walton lived abroad. "I can't say how glad I am that it was not offered to me", he wrote – unconvincingly – to his publisher.

Above: Susana Valeria Rosa Maria Gil Passo as a toddler. She was born on 30 August 1926.

Estancia Elouisa, the Gil family country estate in Argentina. As a child, Susana spent two summer months there every year. She learned to drive the family's station wagon when she was only nine.

Susana (left), with her mother, father and brothers Gonzalo and Harry. Her father, Enrique Gil, was a prominent lawyer in Buenos Aires and was at one time imprisoned by President Perón.

Susana's coming-out dress.

Susana on the family sailing boat.

On the ranch.

First Communion.

Dr. Gil Offers Key To Better Relations

1946: father and daughter on a "Good Neighbour" tour of America. Susana gave a lecture at Vassar College. In Argentina she took a degree as a public translator in English and was working at the British Council when she met Walton.

Below: On board the *Uruguay Star* bound for England. Walton slipped a separate note into Susana's first letter home, reporting that she had caught a cold because of walking about the cabin wearing nothing but her pearl necklace.

NOTICIOSO BRITANICO

Home With a Bride

WILLIAM WALTON, 46-year-old British composer, arrives home at Tilbury to-morrow morning with his South American bride, beautiful Senorita Susana Gil Passo. He went out to South America to attend a composers' conference and met Miss Passo at the British Council building in Buenos Aires. She was social secretary there. They fell in love almost at once.

When the London Symphony Orchestra heard of the romance there was some anxiety as to whether Mr. Walton would be back in time to conduct his music next Tuesday at the Albert Hall. But he cut short his honeymoon to get back.

Evening News, 15 February 1949.

News Chronicle, 29 February 1949. Susana's looks were compared to those of a contemporary Carmen.

Left: Susana in her bridal gown. On their first date Walton said: "You will be very surprised, Miss Gil, to hear that I am going to marry you." "Don't be ridiculous, Dr Walton" she replied. Susana later adapted her wedding dress of white plissé chiffon into an evening gown by cutting off the sleeves. Clothing coupons were still required in post-war London.

The singer and the listener

Carmen wore the red rose—but her costume was black and white. Manchester's Anna Pollak, after only three years as a serious singer, was ready to take the stage at Sadler's Wells in one of opera's most exacting roles last night. As Anna sang, a young señora from Argentina sat in the Albert Hall while her husband conducted his own music. She was Mrs. William Walton, the composer's bride of a month.

Left: The Royal Albert Hall, February 1949. Walton conducts his first concert after his marriage.

Lowndes Cottage, Belgravia, the house bequeathed to Walton by Alice Wimborne.

Sir Kenneth Clark, art historian and administrator and his wife Jane. Walton had an affair with Lady Clark before he married. After Jane had loudly disparaged Susana's dress sense, Susana made her a gift of one of her unwanted wedding presents – a handbag made of green snakeskin.

The entrance hall of Lowndes Cottage. When the Waltons moved to Ischia, they rented out their London home, first to Laurence Olivier and Vivien Leigh and later to the film mogul Harry Saltzman. In 1969 Saltzman produced *The Battle Of Britain*, from which most of Walton's music was cut.

Edith Sitwell, soon to be made a Dame, with the Waltons. The composer's good relations with his first supporters were restored after his marriage, but he disappointed them by going elsewhere for his choice of librettist for his forthcoming opera.

Sacheverell Sitwell at his home, Weston Hall. His books on travel, art and architecture swiftly achieved classic status.

Sir Osbert Sitwell at Montegufoni. He succeeded to the baronetcy in 1943. His five-volume autobiography was published between 1946 and 1950.

Title page of the manuscript of the completed Violin Sonata. The composer withdrew the score for revisions after a tryout performance at the Tonhalle in Zurich in September 1949. He cut a complete movement.

The witty, sharp-tongued sisters Griselda (left) and Diana Gould (later Mrs Kentner and Mrs Menuhin). Walton dedicated his Violin Sonata to them. When Menuhin met the sisters in 1944 he noted admiringly that "they scissored language with incredible rapidity, throwing upon our heads a confetti of fanciful cut-outs and profiles in epigrams". During Alice Wimborne's final illness Griselda had sustained Walton with a racy correspondence. Menuhin's on-off affair with Griselda's elder sister prompted Walton to observe tartly on a postcard "If Yehudi doesn't marry Diana, nobody will."

Yehudi Menuhin and Louis Kentner. They gave the first London performance of Walton's Sonata for Violin and Piano at the Theatre Royal, Drury Lane on 5 February 1950.

Opening page of the printed score of *Façade*. It was finally published in 1951, almost 30 years after the first performance. It was dedicated to Lambert, who died a few weeks later.

Constant Lambert: the last photograph. Years earlier he had joked prophetically that he would write an article about Sir William Walton O.M. by Constant Lambert D.T.

To Constant Lambert

FAÇADE
An Entertainment

Poems by
EDITH SITWELL

Music by
WILLIAM WALTON

FANFARE

Copyright, 1951, by the Oxford University Press, London.   Printed in Great Britain

OXFORD UNIVERSITY PRESS, 44 CONDUIT STREET, LONDON, W. 1

OLDHAM EVENING CHRONICLE, Monday, January 1, 1951.

FOUR LOCAL AWARDS IN HONOURS LIST

William Walton, of Oldham, receives a knighthood

DR. WILLIAM TURNER WALTON, the Oldham-born composer, receives a knighthood in the New Year's Honours List. The List also contains the names of three well-known Oldham men. Councillor H. E. Chamberlain, J.P., and Mr. Harry E. Shaw have been made Members of the British Empire, and Mr. Walter E. Schofield, O.B.E., the Chief Constable, has been awarded the King's Police and Fire Services Medal for distinguished service.

Walton's knighthood, as announced in the *Oldham Chronicle*.

FUNERAL
MR. CONSTANT LAMBERT

The funeral service for Mr. Constant Lambert was held at St. Bartholomew the Great, Smithfield, on Saturday. The Rev. Dr. Newell E. Wallbank officiated. Those present included:—

Mrs. Lambert, Sir William Walton, Mr. Eric Warr, Mr. Edward Clark and Mrs. Clark (Miss Elizabeth Lutyens), Mrs. John Denison, Mr. Reginald Burston, Mr. D. H. Munro, Mr. Michael Wood, Miss Annette Prevost, Miss Ninette de Valois, Mr. Robert Helpmann, Mr. Frederick Ashton, Mrs. Bernard van Dieren, Mrs. Louis Kentner, Mr. Hubert Foss, Mr. Julian Herbage, Mr. Julian Clifford, Mr. and Mrs. Alan Rawsthorne, Mrs. Whitney Smith, Mr. Martin Boddey, Professor E. J. Dent, Mr. Hugo V. Anson, Miss Seymour Whinyates, Mr. E. R. Saxton, Mr. Dallas Bower, and Mrs. Rose Ketchell.

Sir Osbert Sitwell and Miss Edith Sitwell were unable to attend.

Cremation took place at Golders Green.

Lambert's funeral notice, *The Times*, 27 August 1951. He died of drink.

Sir William Walton at his Buckingham Palace investiture, 1951.

The Waltons on the terrace at Casa Cirillo. In her memoirs Susana wrote that Walton declared "it was a good job he had not seen my legs – 'piano legs' – until after the engagement, when it was too late to retreat."

Postcard from Ischia. Among the musicians who visited the island and took the radioactive mud-baths were Herbert von Karajan, Igor Stravinsky and Lennox Berkeley. The Waltons kept open house.

Casa Cirillo, the Waltons' home on Ischia in the 1950s.

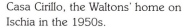

Maria Callas with the Waltons circa 1956. She was Walton's dream casting for the role of Cressida in his new opera.

The Waltons with Spike Hughes and his wife Charmian. The little girl, Maria Esposito, was later in charge of the Waltons' holiday houses.

The composer Hans Werner Henze. When the Waltons met him in 1953 he was living in a peasant's cottage near Casa Cirillo. They initiated him into the delights of the local lobster.

Wystan Auden and Chester Kallman. In the early 1950s they spent each summer in the nearby town of Forio. They collaborated with Stravinsky on *The Rake's Progress*, first given in Venice in 1951. Walton sought their advice about the third act of *Troilus and Cressida*.

The Waltons with more musical friends. The group includes Samuel Barber, Thomas Schippers and Gian-Carlo Menotti.

Manuscript of *Orb and Sceptre*, the 1953 Coronation March.

The 1953 Coronation of Queen Elizabeth II in Westminster Abbey was the first to be televised. Walton's *Coronation Te Deum*, conducted by Dr William McKie, was heard at the end of the ceremony. "You will like it, I think", he had written to Christopher Hassall: "Lots of counter-tenors and little boys Holy-holying, not to mention all the Queen's trumpeters and sidedrums." Walton wore his Oxford Doctor of Music gown. His wife records that "the cream-coloured silk gown, trimmed in shocking fuchsia pink, was temendously *chic* . . . he was outdressed only by the maharajahs from India . . . He filled his round velvet hat . . . with miniature bottles of whisky to sustain himself during the long ceremony".

Recording session for *Orb and Sceptre*, Kingsway Hall, March 1953. Walton conducts the Philharmonia Orchestra. The record was on sale in time for the Coronation that June.

The librettist Christopher Hassall (left) and the conductor Malcolm Sargent (right) gather around the composer and his score for a cosy publicity photograph. But the first orchestral rehearsal was chaotic: Roy Douglas reported 238 errors in the band parts.

Royal Opera House
COVENT GARDEN

THE ROYAL OPERA HOUSE, COVENT GARDEN, LIMITED
GENERAL ADMINISTRATOR . DAVID L. WEBSTER
HOUSE MANAGER . NEVILLE COPPEL

presents

THE WORLD PREMIÈRE OF

Troilus and Cressida

OPERA IN THREE ACTS

Libretto by CHRISTOPHER HASSALL

Music by WILLIAM WALTON

Scenery by HUGH CASSON

Costumes by MALCOLM PRIDE

CONDUCTOR - SIR MALCOLM SARGENT

PRODUCER - GEORGE DEVINE

FRIDAY 3 DECEMBER 1954

The programme for *Troilus and Cressida*, premièred at the Royal Opera House, 3 December 1954.

Rehearsal for *Troilus and Cressida*. Sargent was rather vain and refused to wear his glasses. Walton was disappointed by his evident lack of familiarity with the score.

The soprano Magda László with the composer. The stage at Covent Garden was so cold that Walton's Cressida was obliged to wear a fur coat during rehearsal.

George Devine (1910–1965), actor and stage director. He was entrusted with the production of *Troilus and Cressida* after Laurence Olivier turned the job down in order to direct *Richard III*. Two years later Devine founded the English Stage Company and mounted *Look Back In Anger* at the Royal Court Theatre.

Below: Walton with Walter Legge (1906–1979). Legge was an influential recording producer who admired Walton's music. "It was enough for William to fart for Legge to record it" observed fellow composer Sir Arnold Bax.

David Webster (1903–1971), General Administrator of the Royal Opera House. He had to cope with the late arrival of Walton's score. The première had originally been announced for the 1951–52 Season.

Elisabeth Schwarzkopf. Walton said he wrote the part of Cressida with her voice in mind.

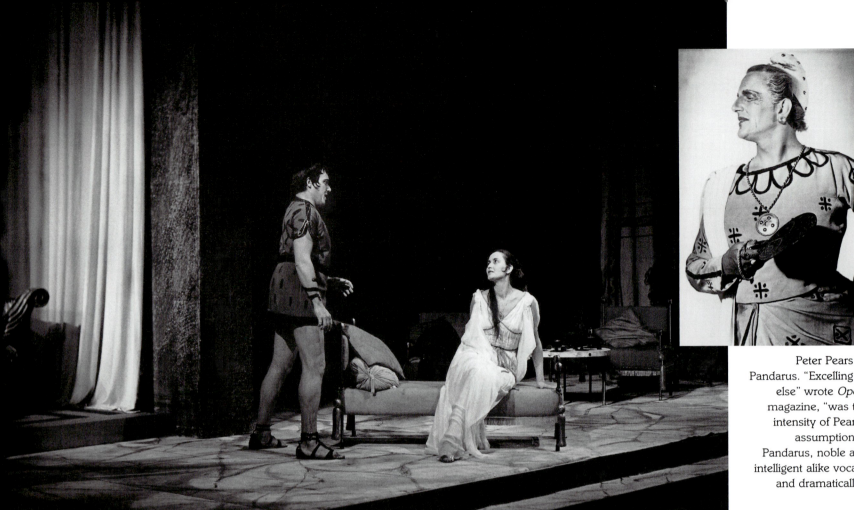

Peter Pears as Pandarus. "Excelling all else" wrote *Opera* magazine, "was the intensity of Pears's assumption of Pandarus, noble and intelligent alike vocally and dramatically".

Richard Lewis as Troilus and Magda László as Cressida.

Set designs for *Troilus and Cressida* by Sir Hugh Casson. He had been knighted in 1952 in recognition of his work for the Festival of Britain. Malcolm Pride designed the costumes.

Daily Mail,
4 December 1954.

A British work the world will watch

WALTON'S OPERA IS A SUCCESS

Daily Express,
4 December 1954.

A NIGHT at the opera

MUSIC COMES OFF ITS HIGH HORSE

OPERA: Troilus and Cressida. THEATRE: Covent Garden.

THE first performance of Sir William Walton's "Troilus and Cressida" last night was the proudest hour for British music since the premiere of Benjamin Britten's "Peter Grimes" nine years ago.

For four years the 52-year-old composer and his librettist, Christopher Hassall, laboured to create an opera worthy of the national opera house. The acclaim of the celebrity-studded first-night audience told them that they had succeeded.

by CECIL SMITH

Three knights were in the group of artists who shared 15 curtain calls at the end of the opera. In addition to Sir William Walton, there were Sir Malcolm Sargent, who conducted at Covent Garden for the first time since 1936, and Sir Hugh Casson, who designed the handsomely proportioned stage settings.

With them were Magda Laszlo, the serenely beautiful Hungarian soprano who sang Cressida, and Richard Lewis, her stalwart, suave-voiced Troilus.

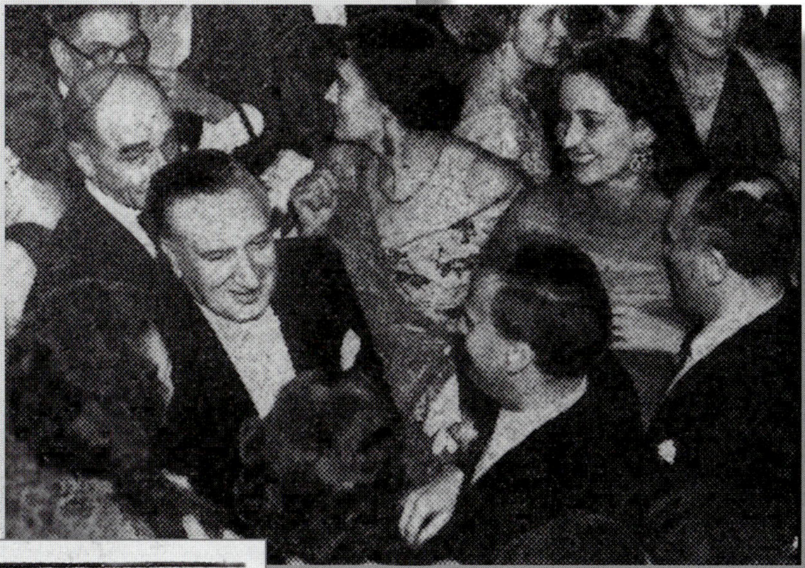

The old Crush Bar of the Royal Opera House. The première of *Troilus and Cressida* was followed by the most glittering first night party since the war. *The Times* review next morning (4 December 1954) hailed "a great tragic opera".

First Nights

WALTON OPERA IS STRONG IN MELODY

Daily Telegraph,
4 December 1954.

Scene from Act I of the La Scala production. Walton said the director, Günther Rennert, was

"splendid, full of imaginative ideas which make everything and everybody become intensely alive and vivid"

The Italian première of *Troilo e Cressida* was given at La Scala, Milan on 12 January 1956.

Act III. The opera was consciously composed in the great Italian operatic tradition and the text was translated by the future Nobel Prize-winner Eugenio Montale. Contemporary reports suggest that the La Scala production was perhaps over-lavish. Susana complained that the great wall of Troy, glimpsed for only a few seconds at the beginning of Act I, masked the voices of the chorus and cost millions of lire that should have been spent on singers.

Post-performance reception in Milan. Left to right: Contessa Castelbarco (Toscanini's daughter), Nicola Benois (set designer), Susana, Walton, Pietro Zuffi (costume designer) and Victor de Sabata (Music Director of La Scala).

Nino Sanzogno, the conductor (left). When Walton took his curtain call he received hisses and boos as well as cheers. Had he had a whistle, Walton said, he would have whistled back.

David Poleri as Troilus and Dorothy Dow as Cressida. In the last scene Cressida is supposed to kill herself with Troilus' sword. "The audience . . . burst into laughter and whistling" Susana reported, when they saw Dorothy Dow "rush around the stage like a hen looking for corn with her head close to her toes, looking for the sword, which had inadvertently been removed."

121

40 years of *Troilus and Cressida*

The 1955 American première at San Francisco Opera. Richard Lewis as Troilus and Dorothy Kirsten as Cressida.

Una Hale assumed the role of Cressida under the bâton of Reginald Goodall when Covent Garden took the opera on a British tour in 1955.

Jill Gomez sang Cressida in a concert performance of Act II at the Royal Albert Hall in a Promenade Concert in 1972. André Previn was the conductor. "As usual you've got it all right." Walton told him after listening to a recording of the broadcast. Previn later pulled out of the 1976 Covent Garden production only days before the start of the rehearsals.

1955 New York City Opera production. Phyllis Curtin as Cressida, Norman Kelley as Pandarus and Jon Crain as Troilus.

1963 Royal Opera House revival. Forbes Robinson as Calkas and Marie Collier as Cressida. Collier also sang Cressida in the Australian première at the Adelaide Festival the following year.

1976 Covent Garden production with Benjamin Luxon as Diomede, Richard Cassilly as the murdered Troilus and Dame Janet Baker as the grieving Cressida.

1995 Opera North production. Arthur Davies as Troilus and Judith Howarth as Cressida.

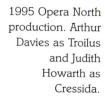

123

"Troilus –
it's a lost child,
if you like."

CHAPTER 7

THE MAKING OF LA MORTELLA

1956–1972

"All bliss consists in this: to do as Adam did."

THOMAS TRAHERNE

WALTON WAS STILL IN THE THROES of his opera when he and Susana moved from their first Ischia home into the nearby Casa Cirillo, a former wine store. Walton completed *Troilus* there and early in 1955 composed the score for Laurence Olivier's third great Shakespeare film, *Richard III*. A sparkling orchestral overture followed, commissioned for the 1956 Johannesburg Festival and he then turned to a new concerto for the violoncello. Walton had decided to put down more substantial roots on Ischia and the commissioning fee was added to the capital of Mrs Courtauld's 1932 bequest in order to acquire a large plot of boulder-strewn hillside terrain a few hundred metres inland from Casa Cirillo. The creation over the next twenty years of the splendid house and garden known as La Mortella – the wild myrtle bush – was to provide Susana (and perhaps William, too) with some degree of emotional compensation for the child they never had together.

Walton was invited to compose his Cello Concerto by the Russian-American cellist Gregor Piatigorsky, a close friend of Jascha Heifetz, who commissioned the Violin Concerto two decades earlier. In his thirties Walton had railed against the tyranny of deadlines and delivery dates but later in life he had no qualms about

At home in Ischia. The dachshund was called Lotti.

Shopping with the Bentley bequeathed to Walton by Alice Wimborne.

composing to order: "I'm a composer. I'll write anything for anybody if he pays me . . . Naturally I write much better if I'm paid in dollars."

In January 1957 the Waltons set off by car for England, intending to attend the London première of the new concerto. On the *autostrada* north of Rome a cement lorry drove across the path of their car and they were both seriously injured in the crash: Walton had a broken hip and Susana suffered a badly gashed forehead, broken ribs and a shattered wrist. During the long weeks of recuperation in hospital, Walton listened to broadcast tapes of the concerto's first performances in Boston and London. He wrote to Piatigorsky, its dedicatee, urging him to make his impending RCA recording "altogether more tough and rhythmical" and when the LP was produced he praised the "absolutely superb interpretation and performance". Critical opinion concerning the concerto was mixed: Peter Heyworth's review dubbed the concerto "run down and enervating" but another critic, Colin Mason, found it "entrancing, a work of a man refreshed in spirit". Heyworth, who became a personal friend despite his hard words, noted (somewhat late in the day) that the *enfant terrible* had become "a pillar of the musical Establishment". Subsequent performance history has established the concerto among the twentieth century's most popular compositions for cello and orchestra (in an admittedly not very large field). Walton told Piatigorsky it was the best of his three concertos, adding "But don't say so to Jascha". A strain of melancholy runs through it but one senses, too, a man at peace with himself. He must have been happy to be relieved of the ardours of collaborating on an opera and supremely content to be married and living with the minimum of fuss on Ischia.

Despite his traumatic accident, Walton was back at work by the spring of 1957, composing a fifteen-minute *Partita for Orchestra*. This was commissioned by the Cleveland Orchestra for its fortieth birthday. It was ready for its première in January 1958 under George Szell and proved to be one of Walton's most instantly attractive post-war orchestral compositions. "It poses no problems," Walton wrote in a programme note, "has no ulterior motives or meaning behind it, and makes no attempt to ponder the imponderable. I have written it in the hope that it may be enjoyed straight

The Waltons with Alan Frank of OUP at the 1960 Edinburgh Festival. Frank is holding the manuscript of the Second Symphony.

off, without any preliminary probing into the score. I have also written it with the wonderful players of the Cleveland Orchestra in mind, hoping that they may enjoy playing it." Walton relished his links with America. He wrote concertos for two world-renowned American soloists and received commissions from no less than five of the leading American orchestras, those of Chicago, Cleveland, New York, San Francisco and Washington (the National Symphony). In 1972 he was awarded the Benjamin Franklin medal for his services to Anglo-American understanding.

Walton's next composition, his Second Symphony, was commissioned in 1956 by the Liverpool Philharmonic Society. Progress was slow and once again he missed a delivery date for a symphony by several years. When the work was eventually premièred by the Royal Liverpool Philharmonic under John Pritchard at the 1960 Edinburgh Festival Walton was unhappy about the inadequate rehearsal conditions – one reason, perhaps, for the work's tepid reception. But the performances given in America the following year by the Cleveland Orchestra under George Szell proved a revelation and after Szell's death Walton re-dedicated the Symphony to his memory. Less raw in its emotions and more tightly organised than its predecessor – it is cast in three movements rather than four – the Second Symphony is the most impressive of Walton's post-war orchestral compositions. Peter Heyworth observed that "there leaps from almost every bar an intense sense of character, compounded of [an] odd assortment of jauntiness, irony and an underlying melancholy."

The theme of the third movement has a striking outline employing all twelve notes of the chromatic scale, as if to show the modernists that he too could produce atonal music if he so desired, but the ten variations, fugue and coda that follow are firmly based in tonality.

Earlier in 1960 the Aldeburgh Festival witnessed the first fruit of the artistic friendship which developed between Walton and the Festival's directors Benjamin Britten and Peter Pears. This was *Anon in Love,* a set of songs for tenor and guitar. The work was dedicated to his friend Lilias Sheepshanks, the first of half a dozen beautiful women to whom Walton was attracted in later life, and inscribed to Pears and Julian Bream, its first interpreters: its six poems by anonymous 16th and 17th century authors were selected for Walton by his librettist Christopher Hassall. (Walton later scored the accompaniments for small orchestra.)

Next Peter Pears suggested a comedy based on a play by Chekhov. Walton replied that there was "nothing that I would like more than to write an opera for the English Opera Group". *The Bear* was initially chosen with the idea of composing the role of the boorish, overbearing Smirnov for Pears himself, a casting against type that would have made an intriguing contrast with Pandarus, the part Pears created in Walton's earlier opera *Troilus and Cressida.* But Pears, well into his fifties, decided he must withdraw and the role was re-cast for baritone. It was originally intended for an Aldeburgh regular, Thomas Hemsley, but eventually created by John Shaw. The libretto for *The Bear* was fashioned by the satirist Paul Dehn. (Christopher Hassall had died unexpectedly in 1963, after running to catch a train to London to attend a performance of *Troilus and Cressida.*) Walton's 45-minute "extravaganza in one act", scored for a small orchestra and employing only three singers, was produced by Colin Graham to great acclaim at the 1967 Aldeburgh Festival. Everybody enjoyed its witty, parodistic score and *The Bear* has since become a mainstay of chamber opera companies around the world. Madame Popova, the delicious young widow with whom Smirnov falls in love, even though he owes her money, was first sung by Monica Shaw; other distinguished interpreters of the role have included the Swedish diva Elisabeth Söderström and the American mezzo Regina Resnik. Unfortunately the recording of the

BBC's television production of the opera – in which Resnik starred – has been lost, presumed "wiped".

In a third composition linked to Aldeburgh, Walton paid direct homage to his younger colleague: his *Improvisations on an Impromptu by Benjamin Britten* date from 1969. They were heard first in San Francisco – the work was commissioned by Dr Stanley Dorfman of that city, in memory of his wife – and then at the newly re-opened Maltings concert hall in Snape under Sir Charles Groves at the 1970 Aldeburgh Festival. Originally they were to be called "elegiac variations" but Dr Dorfman asked for a joyful conclusion to the work, which Walton, ever the professional, duly supplied. The theme for this fascinating set of orchestral variations is taken from Britten's early Piano Concerto.

It was not the first time he had used the variation form to enter into the world of another composer; his *Variations on a Theme of Hindemith* completed in 1963 to a commission from the Royal Philharmonic Society, is second in scale to the Symphony No. 2 among his post-war orchestral works. It was born, he told Britten, "after a prolonged bout of depression . . . my later works always receive such a drubbing from the press, especially my last one [i.e. the Hindemith Variations] which incidentally I consider one of my best." Unlike the friendship with Britten, in which admiration was tinged with a degree of envy (as one may perceive from the occasional mocking "Aldebugger" references in his letters to other friends) his affection for Hindemith was without blemish: forty years had passed since their first meeting as young avant-garde composers at Salzburg. The Variations are dedicated jointly to Hindemith and his wife Gertrud. "We are extremely honoured to find the red carpet rolled out," wrote Hindemith in a warm-hearted letter of thanks,"even on the steps to the back door of fame." Hindemith died later that year, before he could conduct the work himself.

A chance to work again with Osbert Sitwell had gone begging the previous year when Walton rejected a biblical text entitled *Moses and Pharoah* which Sitwell had assembled for a new oratorio to be commissioned by "Uddersfield" (the Huddersfield Choral Society) for its 125th anniversary in 1962. "It's about the plagues and the exodus through the Red Sea", Walton told his publisher Alan Frank; "very Cecil B. de Mille!" So he drew back from a project that might have rivalled *Belshazzar's Feast*, opting instead for a textually more conventional *Gloria,* scored for three soloists, chorus and a large symphony orchestra. Rehearsals for the *Gloria*'s première, conducted by Sargent, were reportedly a shambles, leaving the two men barely on speaking terms. Walton plainly felt the choir had been inadequately rehearsed. Sargent counter-attacked: "the trouble with you, Willie, is that you don't know how to compose." To which Walton replied, witheringly: "the trouble with you Malcolm, is that you don't know how to conduct." (This exchange was reported to the author by an eye-witness, Wyn Morris, conductor of the Huddersfield Choral Society, 1969–74.) The eleven sections of the *Gloria* contain some of Walton's most effective vocal writing. If the work has a shortcoming, it is its brevity, a characteristic shared by all Walton's compositions after *Troilus and Cressida*; its eleven sections last in total a bare twenty minutes. Walton often extolled the merits of concision, preferring the relatively short acts of Puccini and late Verdi operas to the long-winded music dramas of Wagner. But in his pre-war works Walton displayed superb architectural skill in the construction of large forms, notably in the first movement of Symphony No. 1 and the final section of rejoicing (over ten minutes) in *Belshazzar's Feast*. The *Gloria* is performed rather less frequently than it deserves, not because it is difficult to sing – all good choirs enjoy a challenge – but because its brevity gives rise to problems in planning a concert around it.

In the early 1960s the work of taming and cultivating the rocky

The holiday villas at La Mortella.

estate of La Mortella slowly moved forward. First to be prepared was a group of five houses near the road, intended to provide a regular income as lettings during the warm months of the year. The largest holiday villa was named Cristabella, after Lady Aberconway; another was Drina, from the name of Susana's mother Alexandrina. Their occupants were to include such luminaries as Harold Acton, Terence Rattigan, Elsa Schiaparelli and most exotic of all, the Nazi gauleiter Baldur von Schirach, who arrived unheralded within weeks of being released from Spandau prison. The Waltons themselves moved into the house known as San Felice, re-built from a peasant's cottage; Walton took over the converted wine cellar next door as a music room. Russell Page, a noted garden designer, had already drawn up plans for La Mortella's very large garden and in November 1961 work began on the main villa, which was carved out of the side of the hill. With the help of a local engineer the Waltons designed their house themselves; they took up residence in the following August, a few days after the première at the City of London Festival of a second short song cycle by Walton, this time for Elisabeth Schwarzkopf. *A Song for the Lord Mayor's Table* comprised settings of six contrasting poems about London, chosen by Christopher Hassall.

When it was brand new, the house at la Mortella looked so grim the local people called it the barracks, *la caserna,* but creepers, flowering bushes and trees (planted by the hundred at Russell Page's insistence) soon grew up to transform the building and its surroundings into an enchanted corner of the island. Russell Page returned after a decade to create a liquid network of ponds, rivulets and fountains, all served by two huge storage cisterns that had been dug higher up the hillside. Higher still was a swimming-pool looking out on the Mediterranean and reached by a seemingly precarious outdoor electric lift; going up "into the view" on this mini-funicular provided endless pleasure for visitors and hosts alike.

In January 1966 Walton conducted the London première of *The Twelve,* an anthem for choir and orchestra (or organ) to a poem by Wystan Auden – a fellow luminary of Christ Church, Oxford, to which noble institution the ten-minute work was dedicated. A doctor friend noticed that Walton experienced alarming breathing problems after climbing a flight of stairs to a party; an advanced cancer was discovered in the left lung. When he telephoned Susana he joked that since he had only just begun work on *The Bear* "it would not be a great loss if I popped off at this moment, musically speaking." He told Susana to throw away his tobacco and all his precious pipes – he had been an inveterate smoker since his youth, a twenty pipes a day man. After an apparently successful operation and recuperation on Ischia he resumed work on his comic opera, only for the cancer to return in an even more virulent form; a longer, more debilitating radiation treatment followed. Memories of the long-

The Order of Merit

drawn-out suffering of Alice Wimborne began to haunt him. Susana wrote later that exposure to the cobalt rays, applied during daily hospital visits for no less than eleven weeks, burnt the skin on his chest: "This, coupled with the scar from the operation (the surgeon had had to cut William almost in half, to lift the rib cage clear away so he could get at the lung), meant I could no longer hug him . . . The rays had also burnt his oesophagus, which meant he had to eat small quantities of finely cut up food and gradually he even had to give up drinking wine, which he resented very much . . ."

Walton was never the same man again. And yet there was still plenty of zest in his music. *The Bear* was followed by the high spirits of the *Capriccio Burlesco,* commissioned by the New York Philharmonic for its 125th anniversary celebrations and first conducted by André Kostalenetz, an old friend of Susana's family.

In 1967 Walton was deeply touched by his nomination to the Order of Merit, which is limited to twenty-four of the nation's great and good, hand-picked by Her Majesty. "To think that the Queen actually knows I am alive!" he exclaimed when the invitation was hand-delivered to his door. (Britten had received the award two years earlier.) And in 1968 came an invitation to compose the score for a feature film, *The Battle of Britain,* a commission which would help him pay off the debts he had accumulated while creating La Mortella. The film was made in England but with American finance; although the score was swiftly composed and recorded, humiliation followed when the distributing company, United Artists, claimed that Walton's name was not known to them and that there was insufficient music to fill an LP; they insisted on replacing it with music by another composer, Ron Goodwin. After much wrangling and personal pressure from Laurence Olivier, who played Air Marshal Dowding in the film, an unsatisfactory compromise resulted in one substantial section of Walton's music, *The Battle in the Air*, being reinstated but it took three years and the personal intervention of the prime minister, Edward Heath, to persuade the unrepentant film producers to return the composer's manuscript.

The episode made a mockery of Walton's subsequent award from the Royal Society of Arts for his contribution to Anglo–American understanding! But his affection for Laurence Olivier overcame his distaste for the film medium and in 1969 he composed the titles and dream sequence for Olivier's production of *The Three Sisters* by Chekhov. A set of *Five Bagatelles* for Julian Bream's solo guitar followed; he later transcribed them for orchestra under the unwieldy title *Varii Capricci* for performance at the 1976 concert celebrating the 25th anniversary of the opening of the Royal Festival Hall.

In 1971, a year short of his 70th birthday, the London Symphony Orchestra invited Walton to join their tour of the Soviet Union: Susana reports that in Leningrad he was mobbed "by a mass of young people" after a fine performance under André Previn of the First Symphony. But of a new symphony from the composer's pen there was little sign: it seemed he had reached the end of his creative road although another dozen years of mingled depression and hope were still to come.

Walton with André Previn. Previn was a passionate advocate of Walton's orchestral music: Walton particularly admired his recording of the First Symphony, with the London Symphony Orchestra.

The Waltons with Laurence Oliver and his wife Vivien Leigh. They were very close friends. The Waltons sustained Olivier during his wife's bouts of mental illness.

Richard III, 1955, the last of Olivier's Shakespeare films. In 1990 Christopher Palmer fashioned a suite for speaker and orchestra from nine of Walton's musical episodes.

Gregor Piatigorsky (1903–1976) paid Walton $3000 to write a cello concerto, double the fee his friend Jascha Heifetz had been charged for the Violin Concerto back in the 1930s. The world première was given in Boston in January 1957.

Walton composed the Cello Concerto at Casa Cirillo. He wrote to Piatigorsky: "Thank you for everything; your patience, help, kindness, during my writing this work for you, and I only pray it will come up to your high opinion of it."

. . . I am more nervous than you about it."

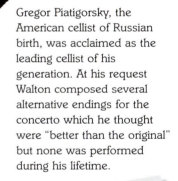

Susana at the wheel. The Waltons were driving to London for the British première of the Cello Concerto when they were involved in a collision with an Italian cement lorry.

Gregor Piatigorsky, the American cellist of Russian birth, was acclaimed as the leading cellist of his generation. At his request Walton composed several alternative endings for the concerto which he thought were "better than the original" but none was performed during his lifetime.

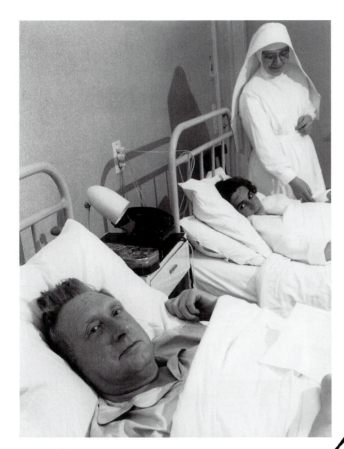

Car crash survivors, January 1957, in adjoining beds in the clinic at Monte Mario, Rome. Walton "agonised over a small radio" in an attempt to hear the London première of his Cello Concerto.

Telegram from Walton to Piatigorsky, 17 January 1957.

Oldham Chronicle, 14 February 1957.

133

Julian Bream and Peter Pears. In 1960 they performed Walton's *Anon In Love* at Shrubland Park Hall in Suffolk as part of the Aldeburgh Festival. Three of the six songs are settings of bawdy seventeenth-century texts in the tradition of Purcell, whose work Pears had done so much to revive.

Bream often visited the Waltons in Ischia. Susana describes him as "short, stubby, pugnacious and funny, with a sense of humour as obstreperous as William's".

Manuscript title page of Walton's *Partita for Orchestra*.

Severance Hall, the home of the Cleveland Orchestra. The *Partita* was first performed there on 13 January 1958.

134

Walton Marks Time

By PETER HEYWORTH

ON Wednesday Sir William Walton's new symphony was brought to town by John Pritchard and the Royal Liverpool Philharmonic Orchestra, who commissioned it.

A new score has a way of falling into clearer perspective when reheard some while after a first performance with all its attendant excitement. Walton's Second Symphony made its bow at this year's Edinburgh Festival, but the intervening months have not enhanced it. The lack of thematic development in the first movement is more apparent, and so is the absence of any strong melodic or harmonic impetus in the lento. The finale wears better, although it does not fulfil the promise of its opening variations. The strength of the work lies in the sense of character that underlies every bar. Walton may lack Fricker's powers of musical organisation, but no one could fail to recognise who this symphony is by.

But the final impression it leaves is of Walton chewing the cud. Does it matter that there is nothing new here, that it marks no advance or

Strauss is an obvious example and I, for one, cannot bring myself to write off all those delicious confections of his decline after the entry of Bacchus in "Ariadne auf Naxos." But there are two things that separate Strauss from Walton. One is that he had much more fat to live off. Like them or not, "Ein Heldenleben" and "Elektra" are clearly the work of a composer built on a larger scale. And then Strauss was a master craftsman. In some of his later operas, such as "Daphne," there is scarcely a whiff of an idea that is not the thinnest dilution of his earlier music. Yet the sheer dexterity with which the old conjurer goes through his tricks carries its own fascination. I wish I felt the same fluency in Walton's new symphony, yet the public clearly enjoyed it intensely, just as they continue to enjoy Strauss in spite of all those critical long noses.

★

THE concert opened with an inadequate account of Mozart's Prague Symphony. Mr. Pritchard breezed through the towering con-

The Observer, 27 November 1960. Peter Heyworth's review of Symphony No. 2. He had previously criticised the Cello Concerto and other recent works of Walton's as showing "no vital development at all". Walton was aghast: "You know, you don't only attack my music, you reduce my income!" Nevertheless, the two men developed a healthy respect for each other and became good personal friends. Walton called Heyworth his "tormentor-in-chief".

John Pritchard (1921–1989), Conductor of the Royal Liverpool Philharmonic Orchestra, examines the score of Symphony No. 2 with the composer. Preliminary rehearsals were held in a schoolroom, where orchestral balance was difficult to judge. The première was given in the Usher Hall, Edinburgh on 2 September 1960. Critical reception was mixed and EMI cancelled the recording sessions it had planned.

George Szell (1897–1970) with the Concertgebouw Orchestra in Amsterdam conducting the European première of Walton's Symphony No. 2. To have the enthusiastic support of one of the world's leading conductors was a great solace when British critics were so unappreciative.

Walton with Szell. The Hungarian-born conductor recorded the Symphony No. 2 with the Cleveland Orchestra in 1962. Walton was delighted with Szell's interpretation, calling it "a quite fantastic and stupendous performance from every point of view".

The Huddersfield Choral Society, one of Britain's outstanding vocal ensembles. Walton composed his *Gloria* for the Society's 125th birthday and Malcolm Sargent's 30th anniversary as its conductor.

WILLIAM WALTON

GLORIA

Vocal Score

OXFORD UNIVERSITY PRESS

Walton later doubted whether his *Gloria* was "worth the hard labour necessary to really make it come off".

Walton is joined by Malcolm Sargent and Chorus Master Herbert Bardgett at the première of *Gloria* on 24 November 1961.

1961: the return to his birthplace of the Prodigal Son. Despite the headline none of his subsequent compositions was dedicated to Oldham.

OLDHAM EVENING CHRONICLE, Wednesday, April 19, 1961

'HIS GENIUS REFLECTS GREAT LUSTRE ON OLDHAM'—CIVIC LEADER

Sir William receives freeman honour
TO DEDICATE MUSIC TO TOWN OF HIS BIRTH

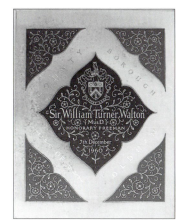

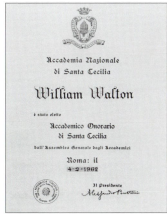

1961: illuminated manuscript granting Walton the Freedom of the town. Oldham was careful with its honours: Walton was only the fourteenth Freeman in over a century.

Walton's certificate of Honorary Membership of the Accademia Nazionale di Santa Cecilia in Rome.

" Critics ? I shall confine myself to physical assault "

William Walton

Sunday Telegraph, 26 March 1962.

My Life in Music

The composer of 'Façade' and 'Belshazzar's Feast,' 60 this week, writes for the first time of how he arrived, the personalities of his time, today's avant-garde–and the critics.

By Sir WILLIAM WALTON

137

"On these rocks we must build"

decreed the composer, seen (right) with Susana amid the trees in the garden of La Mortella.

The view from the hillside of Monte Zaro. Villa La Mortella was built on its slope.

Russell Page, the noted British landscape artist. He drew up the plan for the wild rock garden of La Mortella. He advised the planting of sturdy young trees to withstand the winter gales and the building of dry and straight stone walls to hold the earth in place on the hillside.

1963: The Waltons leaving the Chelsea Flower Show, laden with plants and bulbs for La Mortella.

Susana on the steps of La Mortella; next to her is a bush of the wild myrtle, from which the estate took its name.

The Waltons in their new garden with Mount Epomeo in the background.

A photo-call at La Mortella required evidence of the composer's physical involvement . . .

on the road . . .

In the 1963–64 season Walton undertook several conducting tours to raise money for La Mortella.

Lewisohn Stadium was the leading open-air venue for summer concerts in New York City between 1918 and 1966. It held well over 20,000 people. Walton also conducted at Ravinia Park, outside Chicago.

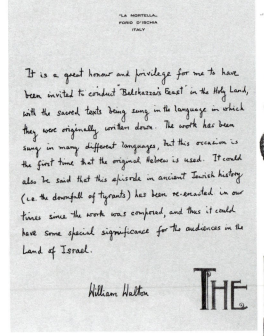

It is a great honour and privilege for me to have been invited to conduct "Belshazzar's Feast" in the Holy Land, with the sacred texts being sung in the language in which they were originally written down. The work has been sung in many different languages, but this occasion is the first time that the original Hebrew is used. It could also be said that this episode in ancient Jewish history (i.e. the downfall of tyrants) has been re-enacted in our times since the work was composed, and thus it could have some special significance for the audiences in the Land of Israel.

William Walton

Letter from the composer to members of the Israel Philharmonic Orchestra.

Belshazzar's Feast was translated into Hebrew for the July 1963 Israel Festival.

Walton with his sister Nora Donnelly. They were reunited when he conducted in New Zealand in 1964. They had rarely met since the days when he used to push her down the hill on a tea tray.

Famous composer feted at parties

THERE'S a round of parties in progress for visiting composer and conductor, Sir W... in a two-... to Sydney...

Part and parcel of a celebrated musician's life on tour. Susana had broken her leg and was unable to accompany her husband on the world tour they had planned. She received no word from him for several months. "When he arrived home", Susana wrote in her memoirs, "he was amazed to learn that I had not had a letter from him as he had written regularly . . . [He] told me he had consoled himself while away not with Australian beauties but by visiting as many Australian botanical gardens as he could find".

Stepping up to the podium in Queensland.

With friends and admirers in Sydney.

Kerrie the Koala: the obligatory Australian photo-call.

"... I must admit to have been suffering from a prolonged bout of depression ..."

Manuscript of *Variations on a Theme by Hindemith*. The theme was taken from the second movement of Hindemith's Cello Concerto.

Paul and Gertrud Hindemith. The *Variations* were dedicated to them. The work was commissioned for the 150th birthday of the Royal Philharmonic Society.

Letter to Benjamin Britten, 2 January 1964. He refers in it to his Hindemith Variations.

Walton in 1966.

Wystan Auden (1907–1973) collaborated with Walton on *The Twelve*, an Anthem for the Feasts of the Apostles.

Daily Telegraph, 9 February 1966. The headline proved unduly optimistic: Walton suffered a second attack of cancer the following spring. He beat the illness but lost half of one lung.

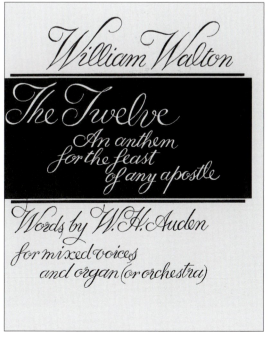

.E, Wednesday, February 9, 1966.

CANCER CURED —SIR WILLIAM TO DO AN OPERA

THE Oldham-born composer, Sir William Walton, is to start work on a new opera—just a few weeks after a lung cancer operation.

Sir William, a freeman of the borough, had the operation at the London Clinic three weeks ago, it was revealed this week.

He said last night: "I went to a doctor for another reason and he discovered there was a shadow on my lung—it was a cancer at a rather young stage.

"I had it nipped out in the London Clinic. It was a major operation and it was 100 per cent successful. It was just common or garden cancer."

The 63-year-old composer added that he was feeling "all right now" and would resume work on a new opera, "The Bear," for the English Opera Group when he returned to his home on the Italian island of Ischia at the end of the month.

Letter from Auden to Walton, 22 December 1964. A few days later, writing to his publisher, Walton described the poem as "a somewhat obscure and difficult-to-set text".

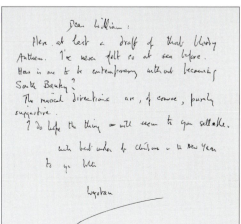

The Twelve was first performed at Christ Church, Oxford on 16 May 1965. An orchestral version celebrated the 900th anniversary of the founding of Westminster Abbey the following January.

William Walton

The Twelve
An anthem for the feast of any apostle

Words by W. H. Auden for mixed voices and organ (or orchestra)

What are you at now?
I have always thought you should do a short Tchehov (The Bear or The Proposal) as a Comic 1-act Opera for the English Opera Group. Why don't you?!
Love to Sue and from Ben
Yours ever Peter

Letter from Peter Pears to Walton,
5 November 1964.

John Shaw created the role of Smirnov the Bear at the 1967 Aldeburgh Festival.

Paul Dehn (1912–1976), librettist of Walton's comic one-act opera *The Bear*. Film critic and lyricist, Dehn wrote libretti for two operas by Lennox Berkeley. Walton met him through the playwright Terence Rattigan. For Walton's 70th birthday Dehn composed an *Ode* including the immortal couplet:

"And the air on Ischia
Seems to make you friskier."

144

The Bear:

"I have become so used to being slated by those critics that I felt there must be something wrong when the worms turned on some praise."

Håkan Hagegård and Elisabeth Söderström in a Swedish Royal Opera production of *The Bear*.

Walton at the original-cast recording of *The Bear* in December 1967. Monica Sinclair took the role of Madame Popova.

The Bear is a favourite with chamber groups the world over and has been translated into many languages.

Letter to Benjamin Britten,
9 September 1968.

At the rebuilt Maltings
Concert Hall, Snape,
Sir Charles Groves conducts a
rehearsal of *Improvisations
on an Impromptu of
Benjamin Britten*. The work
was first performed at the
1970 Aldeburgh Festival.

Benjamin Britten. He responded by return of post when Walton
requested permission to use one of his themes as the basis for a
new orchestral work.

The theme from Britten's Piano Concerto selected by Walton for his *Improvisations*.

Walton greeted by Yehudi Menuhin at EMI's Abbey Road Studios. Together they recorded Walton's concertos for viola and violin. Menuhin told Susana that he had given up the violin for a month before recording the Viola Concerto, in order to accustom his fingers to the larger instrument. The *Gramophone* review of the Violin Concerto commented that Menuhin was on top form "for Walton's dreamily romantic melodies and apparently undaunted by the passages of double- and triple-stopped scraping".

When Menuhin later repeated his interpretation of the Viola Concerto at the Royal Festival Hall (with the LSO under Previn) the *Financial Times* critic Ronald Crichton noted that Menuhin's viola had such a penetrating tone that "one wished that just this once they had gone back to the old scoring with triple wind and without harp – no doubt the revisions [of 1961] make life easier for the solo, but the smoothing and streamlining tone down an acerbity that was very much part of the music, while the harp brings it nearer the Tennysonian euphony of Ischia and [Walton's] later period, very beautiful yet different."

Walton with André Kostelanetz, the celebrated conductor of light classical music. Susana's father had represented him in South America. Kostelanetz was in charge of the New York Philharmonic's summer promenade concerts.

Concert programme for the 1968 world première of Walton's *Capriccio Burlesco*, commissioned by the New York Philharmonic Orchestra to celebrate its 125th anniversary.

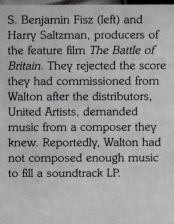

Film-makers Scorn Walton's Score

SIR WILLIAM WALTON, O.M. tells me he will never again write a bar of film music. "I have been treated," he says, "in the most extraordinary way."

Commissioned last August by Spitfire Productions to write the music for their film *Battle of Britain*, [he] worked on the sc[ore at his h]ouse on the [island] of Ischia unt[il it] was then reco[rded at] Elstree Studios u[nder the baton] of Mal[colm Arnold, a] fellow

Sunday Telegraph,
22 June 1969.

Laurence Olivier as Air Chief Marshall Sir Hugh Dowding in *The Battle of Britain*. Olivier threatened to remove his name from the film credits unless some of Walton's music was restored.

"Battle in the Air" was the only sequence of Walton's music to be retained in the film.

S. Benjamin Fisz (left) and Harry Saltzman, producers of the feature film *The Battle of Britain*. They rejected the score they had commissioned from Walton after the distributors, United Artists, demanded music from a composer they knew. Reportedly, Walton had not composed enough music to fill a soundtrack LP.

Recording session at Denham Studios. Malcolm Arnold (left), seen here with Walton and the film's director Guy Hamilton, conducted the session at Walton's invitation. The composer took over for the March. An eyewitness, Edward Greenfield, noted that "the first three notes may be a blatant crib from the opening of Elgar's Second Symphony, but they turn at once into the purplest Walton". Malcolm Arnold (born 1921) was one of Walton's closest friends.

The Three Sisters. In 1969 Laurence Olivier directed the film version of his National Theatre production. Walton provided music for the titles and a six-minute dream sequence. Left to right: Joan Plowright (Olivier's second wife and a frequent visitor at La Mortella) as Masha, Louise Purnell as Irina and Jeanne Watts as Olga.

Laurence Olivier as Dr Chebutikin in *The Three Sisters*. It was Walton's last music for film.

42

NEWS IN BRIEF

by LESLIE GEDDES-BROWN

'Battle' music flies again

SIR WILLIAM WALTON'S lost and unheard music for the film "The Battle of Britain", which disappeared in 1969, will be premièred next year when EMI releases the second of two albums of the composer's film music by the Liverpool Philharmonic under Sir Charles Groves.

Sunday Times, 13 March 1983.
The EMI recording project foundered but the *Suite from The Battle of Britain*, arranged by the composer Colin Matthews, was premièred in 1985 and later recorded under Carl Davis.

André Previn (the American conductor, jazz pianist and composer, born in 1929) was principal conductor of the London Symphony Orchestra 1969–79. He appeared frequently on BBC Television and used his popular appeal to promote the cause of British music, notably that of Walton and Vaughan Williams.

Above: Leningrad, 1971, after André Previn had conducted the London Symphony Orchestra in a performance of Walton's First Symphony. The audience had been unaware of Walton's presence and immediately started cheering. Susana remembers that "he was mobbed . . . surrounded by a mass of young people [who] climbed on to each other's shoulders to get a glimpse of him".

After the First Symphony had been repeated in Moscow, the British Ambassador patted Walton on the back saying: "Not bad this. Have you written anything else?"

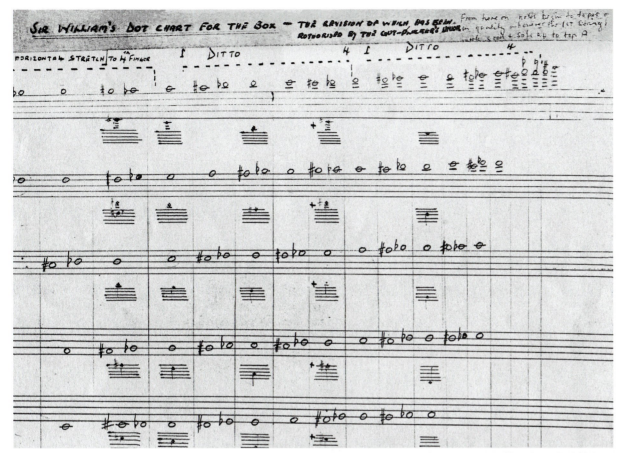

Julian Bream's guide to the guitar, prepared especially for Walton. "Never having thought of writing for the guitar," Walton said, "I asked Julian for a chart explaining what the guitar could do."

Walton composed his *Five Bagatelles* in 1971. Bream gave the first performance of the first three on BBC Television on Walton's 70th birthday. The work was later dedicated to Malcolm Arnold "with admiration and affection".

Walton with Julian Bream. Walton later upbraided Bream for not playing his *Bagatelles* often enough. Bream says he left the room "with the distinct impression that he thought I'd been pulling a fast one".

'...the boy from Oldham marvelled at
having achieved his goal: to live
surrounded by grounds full of flowering
bushes and lemon trees." Susana Walton from *Behind the Façade*

CHAPTER 8

THE GRAND OLD MAN

1972–1983

The composer with his bust sculpted by Elizabeth Frink, 1976.

"I'm looking forward to all the fuss." WALTON

THE BRITISH ARTS ESTABLISHMENT likes nothing better than to celebrate an anniversary. Walton was chronically insecure but the festive celebrations for his 70th birthday, extending over six months, provided at least temporary reassurance that he was held in high esteem. At the televised Royal Festival Hall concert André Previn conducted *Belshazzar's Feast*, Yehudi Menuhin repeated his fine interpretation of the Viola Concerto (already recorded for EMI four years previously) and a group of younger composers, among them Nicholas Maw and Peter Maxwell Davies, contributed a set of variations on Happy Birthday to You! "A real tribute from the avant-garde to the almost buried and dead" was Walton's caustic appraisal. His decline and creative impotence were to be the burden of many letters from Ischia in his final decade.

But these at least were glory days. The prime minister of the day, Edward Heath, did something unheard of in modern times: he arranged a party for a composer at 10 Downing Street, attended by the Queen Mother. The climax of the evening, close to midnight, was the performance of a work Walton had confided to Mr Heath he wished he had composed himself, Schubert's Piano Trio in B flat. The guests from the arts fraternity's upper echelons included Kenneth Clark and his wife Jane, Walton's old flame. Earlier the party had been entertained by an Ode composed by the Master of the Queen's Music, Sir Arthur Bliss, to words by Paul Dehn. It enumerated Walton's achievements, citing

> Concertos written by this fertile fellow
> For violin, viola and cello,
> *Troilus and Cressida* – sad pursuant pair –
> Pursued, a decade later, by *The Bear*.
> Prince Hamlet, Richard Crookback, Henry Five
> (Graced by his music track) became alive.

And still his Overtures and his *Façade*
Quicken the feet of those who promenade.

But composition became an ever more painful process. "I am . . . completely horrified at my impotence", he told Roy Douglas, his music editor and friend of forty years' standing. "I've come to face that I've no real necessity to write anything any more. After all, better composers than myself stopped, Verdi for instance soon after 70 and didn't start again till he was about 78 or so." "If one's not careful", he told a journalist, "one tends to become repetitious; an idea comes into your head and you find it's the same one you had ten years ago. Then I see the headline: 'Walton makes no progress.' I do believe that a composer must stay true to himself. I don't believe in trying to keep up with every fashion as Stravinsky tried to do. It's like having your face lifted." (*The Times* 13 November 1976)

Many of his grumbles, good-humoured for the most part, but with an occasional hint of desperation, fell on the ears of Diana Rix, the vivacious administrator of his musical engagements at the Harold Holt concert agency. "I'm alright", he told her, "but my muse ain't. She's like you – shows no signs of giving in". He was rash enough to promise the London Symphony Orchestra a third symphony and sketched the opening bars on a page of manuscript which he sent to his friend and champion André Previn. Fifty years earlier the musical world had waited in vain for Jean Sibelius to deliver an eighth symphony. In his turn Walton wearily conceded defeat. ("Alright for him, he'd already done seven . . . I've only written two.") The music he did manage to compose in his seventies was hardly taxing, consisting for the most part of ceremonial fanfares and short choral works to religious texts, the most significant being the *Cantico del Sole,* to a text by St Francis of Assisi. But he continued to compose every morning and took a keen business interest in the propagation of his work. Despite money worries (engendered by borrowing to the hilt in order to develop the estate of La Mortella) he and Susana led what he described as "a comfortable existence: I get a good, even fat income from the PRS and the OUP". A fellow composer, John Ireland, once described him as "the most mercenary-minded composer I have ever met" but that verdict is harsh; he was certainly Lancashire canny and fanatical in pursuit of performances of his music but he was also generous with gifts to his friends and encouragement to his younger composer colleagues.

In her memoirs Susana Walton relates that her husband never lost his eye for a good-looking woman. Some she sent packing; others she not merely tolerated but actively disarmed – by herself offering the hand of friendship. She learnt to accept that while Walton was grappling with a composition he had to be entirely self-centred. "When he worked, we met at mealtimes, took an afternoon walk, and slept in the same bed, but rarely communicated . . . between works we had hilarious and happy times."

Artistically, the most disappointing event of his seventies was the new production of *Troilus and Cressida* undertaken by the Royal Opera House in 1976. When a revival was first contemplated early in the decade Walton rightly suggested that Placido Domingo and Kiri te Kanawa, then at the beginning of their careers, could play the title roles to perfection: instead he unwisely allowed himself to be persuaded to transpose the soprano role down for the mezzo Janet Baker, a superb singer but arguably a little mature for the part of Cressida. Walton was not alone in feeling that the American tenor eventually chosen for Troilus was mis-cast. The stage director Colin Graham recalls that the production was allocated only £15,000, less than a tenth of what was spent the same season on Puccini's *Girl of the Golden West*. Sets and costumes were recycled from stock in the opera house storerooms. The conductor

was to have been André Previn (who had never conducted an opera) but he withdrew under doctor's orders only a week before rehearsals were due to begin, pleading an attack of bursitis. Another American, Lawrence Foster, was selected to replace him, a bewildering choice since he had to learn the work at exceptionally short notice. Obliged to be in London for the month-long rehearsal period the Waltons could not afford the Savoy and stayed instead at an Aldwych hotel which was close to Covent Garden but according to Susana smelt perpetually of cabbages. Walton felt badly let down by the Royal Opera, complaining that "they are afraid of flying high", and under the protracted tension of the rehearsals his health faded visibly: at the party after the first performance he collapsed. He returned immediately to Ischia, where Susana and the housekeeper Reale nursed him devotedly for three months, but during his nervous breakdown he suffered hallucinations; in one he was being eaten alive by insects, in another burned alive in an aeroplane which he was forced to pilot. Susana recalled that "it would take quite a time to wake him and convince him he was in his own bed and not in a burning plane. Only by massaging his legs could I prove to him that he was not being attacked".

Reale Patalano, the housekeeper
at La Mortella.

Ironically his illness occurred as his fame was approaching its zenith, thanks in part to a succession of substantial television programmes. As early as 1968, BBC-2 had made its first Walton documentary. Normally such films offer a respectful *tour d'horizon*, but this one aroused the composer's ire when he viewed the "rough-cut" because John Warrack's narration gave the impression (according to Walton) that his post-war works were "hardly worth-while mentioning". Intense pressure from Ischia resulted in the BBC withdrawing the offending passage before transmission. In 1975 a feature on ITV's *Aquarius* programme offered a more sympathetic portrait of Walton, interviewed by Russell Harty. The camera also eavesdropped on a Mediterranean meeting with a fellow Lancastrian, the flamboyant singer and entertainer Gracie Fields, who lived on the nearby island of Capri. For his 75th birthday two years later BBC Television made amends for its earlier *faux pas* with two linked programmes, an *Omnibus* biography and a fine studio performance by the London Symphony Orchestra under Previn of the First Symphony. ITV's *South Bank Show* went one better in 1981 with a vivid documentary portrait by Tony Palmer entitled *At the Haunted End of the Day* (the opening line of Cressida's aria in Act II of *Troilus and Cressida*). The film covered every significant section of his life and music, including a dramatic reconstruction of the traumatic journey with his mother to the Oxford choral audition in 1912; another unusual sequence showed the Grimethorpe Colliery Band playing Walton's own newly-completed transcription of his music for the C.B. Cochran revue, *The First Shoot.* Tony Palmer obtained the Waltons' full collaboration and the enthusiastic participation of friends and collaborators, led by Sir Laurence Olivier; the film was later awarded the Italia Prize for the best music documentary of the year and was subsequently transmitted in thirty-five countries. (It is still projected continuously during visiting hours in the Walton Museum at La Mortella.)

In 1980 Walton accepted two commissions from Mstislav Rostropovitch, whom he had met at Aldeburgh: a *Passacaglia* for solo cello and a concert work, *Prologo e Fantasia,* for Rostropovitch's orchestra, the National Symphony of Washington. Work on the latter composition was dogged by bad health; he suffered from cataracts in both eyes and his legs became so weak that there were days, he wrote, when he could "hardly walk even from the pfte to my desk". Rostropovitch performed both works in London in the weeks preceding Walton's 80th birthday in March 1982; they were received respectfully but with no great stir. Michael Kennedy writes of the *Prologo* that its perfunctory conclusion, "just when one is hoping for an extended coda, is frustrating – and from it we may infer the tragic bewilderment pervading Walton's creative struggle at this period". A spectacular birthday concert relayed by BBC Television from the Royal Festival Hall provided almost the last public view of Walton. Gaunt and frail, he had tears in his eyes as with great difficulty he struggled to his feet in the royal box to acknowledge the audience's overwhelming ovation. A few days later the extended birthday celebrations, which involved concerts in Oxford, Westminster Abbey and the newly-opened Barbican Centre, triggered another physical and nervous breakdown and more alarming hallucinations.

After his recovery Walton agreed as a jape to appear in a feature film, dressing up in royal finery to play the cameo, non-speaking rôle of the venerable King of Saxony in Tony Palmer's epic life of Richard Wagner. The balcony terrace at La Mortella was transformed for the day into a film studio. Walton's part was, he said, a nice piece of typecasting on Palmer's part: it required of him nothing more arduous than to fall asleep while listening to Wagner's music.

Walton was to make only one more visit to London, to receive treatment for cataracts in both his eyes; the second operation went badly and led to a further spell in an intensive care unit. Back on Ischia, and with his debts finally paid off, Walton told his wife he would travel no more: "it was now time to let the music speak for itself", she recalled, "We felt safe, rejoiced over being together, able to enjoy our joint creation, La Mortella". His last composing activity was to write a new coda for the orchestral version of his *Five Bagatelles*, originally composed for Julian Bream's guitar and now chosen by Frederick Ashton for a ballet to be danced by the Royal Ballet led by Anthony Dowell and Antoinette Sibley.

His death came suddenly, only days after the work was completed. On March 5th, just three weeks before his 81st birthday, he awoke complaining of breathlessness. The local doctor gave him a gentle booster for his heart, as he had done on previous occasions, and reassured him that he would soon feel better. Susana and Reale propped him up on his pillows. "Don't leave me, please don't leave me", he said to his wife. Five minutes later she felt him shake with a slight tremor and he died instantly; the doctor was still in the room writing out a prescription. The body was taken to Florence for cremation and in July a memorial service was held in Westminster Abbey. Afterwards Susana unveiled a black stone embedded in the floor of the abbey's Musicians' Corner. It is inscribed, in simple white letters, *William Walton* OM. At La Mortella the composer's ashes are preserved in what is known as "William's Rock", a large pyramid-shaped stone that once served as a boundary marker on a pathway high above the house, looking out over the Bay of Naples. Susana herself composed its inscription:

Sing a song of praise
Beloved and revered master
This rock holds his ashes
The garden he surveys
Russell Page designed
Together we happily
Brought it to life

SUSANA

"All bliss consists in this:
To do as Adam did"

TRAHERNE 1637–1674

157

It's Waltonia in London!

Evening Standard, 6 March 1972, previewing Walton's 70th birthday celebrations.

29 March 1972. 70th birthday party at 10 Downing Street. The Waltons are welcomed by HRH Queen Elizabeth The Queen Mother and the prime minister, Edward Heath.

Dinners

Prime Minister

Queen Elizabeth the Queen Mother was present at a dinner given by the Prime Minister at 10 Downing Street last evening for Sir William and Lady Walton on the occasion of Sir William's seventieth birthday. Among those present were: The Earl and Countess of Drogheda, Viscount and Viscountess Eccles, Lord Goodman, Lord and Lady Clark, Lord Boyle of Handsworth, Baroness Lee of Asheridge, Lord and Lady Olivier, Lord and Lady Zuckerman, Mr John Peyton, MP, and Mrs Peyton, the Hon John and Dame Olivia Mulholland, Sir Arthur and Lady Bliss, Sir Georg and Lady Solti, Sir Thomas and Lady Armstrong, Sir Thomas and Lady Holmes Sellors, Dr and Mrs Malcolm Arnold, Mr and Mrs David Atherton, Mr Richard Rodney Bennett, Mr Benjamin Britten, Mr Paul Dehn, Mr and Mrs Bryan Forbes, Mr and Mrs Alan Frank, Dr Herbert Howells, Miss Ursula Howells, Dr and Mrs John Hunt, Mr and Mrs Ian Hunter, Mr and Mrs Alvar Lidell, Mr and Mrs Yehudi Menuhin, Mr Russell Page, Mrs Alan Rawsthorne, Dr Jean Shanks, Captain and Mrs Robin Sheepshanks, Mr and Mrs Lionel Tertis, Mr and Mrs John Tooley, Mr and Mrs Alec Walton and Mr and Mrs Robert Armstrong

The Times, 30 March 1972.

Telegram from Laurence Olivier with the suggested text of Walton's after-dinner birthday speech at No.10. Instead of learning it by heart, Walton read it out verbatim.

DEAR BOY THIS NO JOKING IS YOUR SPEECH AND IS SENT YOU HEREWITH TO GIVE YOU CHANCE TO LEARN IT SO THAT YOU KNOW IT ABSOLUTELY BY HEART WITH NO WORRIES STOP EDIT IT OF COURSE DO ANYTHING YOU WANT WITH IT DONT USE IT AT ALL BUT I PROMISED TO DO THIS FOR YOU AND HERE IT IS QUOTE LADIES AND GENTLEMEN YOU WILL UNDERSTAND I HOPE THAT IT IS EXTREMELY DIFFICULT FOR ME TO SPEAK ON THIS OCCASION FOR THE VERY SIMPLE REASON THAT IT IS BEYOND THE CONDUCT OF THIS MEDIUM OF SPEECH OR THE CONTROL OF HUMAN EMOTION THAT TRUE EXPRESSION CAN BE FOUND FOR MY FEELINGS I BEG YOU TO FORGIVE ME AND TO UNDERSTAND THAT I AM MADE HAPPY BEYOND WORDS BY YOUR EXTRAORDINARY KINDNESS AND GENEROSITY WITH WHICH BEING MATCHLESS IT IS NOT POSSIBLE FOR ME TO COMPETE I THANK GOD FOR MAKING ME SEVENTY SO THAT YOU COULD MAKE ME SO HAPPY

Menu card designed by Sir Hugh Casson.

A Birthday Grace by Herbert Howells written for the occasion.

"The Happy Birthday Team".
Six composers contributed
to the LSO's 70th birthday
tribute at the Royal Festival
Hall, 28 March 1972.
Left to right:
André Previn (conductor),
Richard Rodney Bennett,
Thea Musgrave, Walton,
Robert Simpson, Peter
Maxwell Davies, Nicholas
Maw and Malcolm Arnold.

At the Royal Northern
College of Music 1972,
where Walton received
an Honorary Doctorate.
With him is his
biographer, Michael
Kennedy.

Manchester, 1972. Walton was reunited with his brothers Alec (left) and Noel (right).

159

The opening five bars of Walton's projected third symphony. No other sketches have survived. This page was sent to the conductor André Previn with the following inscription: "Dear André Here are a few – very few – bars which I hope will eventually turn out to be Symphony III – We'll see! William 3.1.74"

Walton, then aged 74, with the American conductor Lawrence Foster, who took over the 1976 performances of *Troilus and Cressida* after André Previn withdrew at short notice. Walton collapsed on the opening night.

The Royal Opera House's 1976/77 Season brochure announced the new production of *Troilus and Cressida*.

Richard Cassilly as Troilus and Janet Baker as Cressida. She had just been appointed a Dame of the British Empire.

Colin Graham in rehearsal. He had already directed *The Bear* and was devoted to Walton. The composer adapted the score to accommodate the mezzo timbre of Janet Baker. But the low-budget production disappointed him and left some critics cold. "Have I got to be frank?" wrote Bayan Northcott in the *Sunday Telegraph* (21 November 1976); "there were moments . . . when I caught myself wondering why on earth Covent Garden was bothering itself at all with such a hopeless old dodo as *Troilus and Cressida.*"

from the North
GRANADA
PRESENTS

On-screen symbol of Granada Television. Every day between 1965 and 1973 Walton's music, a five-minute march arranged for Symphonic Wind Band by Gilbert Vintner, accompanied the starting up of the television transmitters. The original version, re-named *Prelude For Orchestra*, received its première in 1977 with the Young Musicians' Symphony Orchestra under James Blair.

Radio Times billing for the 1972 BBC Television tribute.

Walton at 70

An affectionate tribute to **Sir William** on his birthday from some of his friends Introduced by **John Amis** with excerpts from *Façade* with **Fenella Fielding Michael Flanders** and the Nash Ensemble directed by **Marcus Dods** and *Bagatelles* (1971) for guitar played by **Julian Bream.** **Hans Keller** and **Richard Rodney Bennett** pay tribute in words. **Malcolm Arnold Hans Werner Henze, André Previn** and **Malcolm Williamson** pay tribute in music specially composed for this occasion and performed by **Yehudi Menuhin, André Previn Thomas Hemsley** and others

Director ROY TIPPING
Producer JOHN AMIS
(Composing has always been a nightmare for me: page 15)

Façade was televised from the Proms in *Music On Two*, BBC-2, 1965, with the composer conducting. Hermione Gingold (pictured above) shared the recitation with Russell Oberlin.

Face the Music. "Popular Song" from *Façade* was used as the signature tune for this popular, long-running BBC Television entertainment. Left to right: Robin Ray, quizmaster Joseph Cooper and Joyce Grenfell. Walton himself appeared twice as a guest on the programme.

The Bear, televised by the BBC in 1969, starred Thomas Hemsley (Smirnov) and Regina Resnik (Popova). Walton himself conducted. The role of Smirnov was composed with Hemsley's voice in mind.

Workshop, the 1968 BBC-2 profile. Walton is seen here with Peter Pears and Cleo Laine, who recited *Façade*.

"Sir William and Our Gracie", *Aquarius*, London Weekend Television, 1976. A trio of Lancastrians; left to right: Dame Gracie Fields, interviewer Russell Harty and Walton.

Laurence Olivier and Peter Hall in front of the newly built National Theatre on London's South Bank. Walton wrote a *Fanfare for the National* for Derek Bailey's documentary *Your National Theatre*, London Weekend Television, 1976.

Sir William Walton, OM, is 80 today. Once the 'enfant terrible' of British music, now its Grand Old Man, he celebrates his birthday at 8.0 pm

8.0 pm
Sir William Walton's
80th Birthday Concert
live from the
Royal Festival Hall, London
conducted by **André Previn**
in the presence of
HRH Princess Alexandra and
The Composer
Kyung-Wha Chung (violin)
Thomas Allen (baritone)
Philharmonia Chorus
guest chorus-master
ANDREW GREENWOOD
Philharmonia Orchestra
leader CHRISTOPHER WARREN-GREEN
Music by **William Walton**
Part 1: Anniversary Fanfare
Coronation March: Orb and Sceptre
Violin Concerto
8.45° Interval
A biographical interlude written
by GILLIAN WIDDICOMBE, with com-
ments from SIR WILLIAM WALTON.
Director HAZEL WRIGHT
9.5° Part 2: Belshazzar's Feast
Introduced by CORMAC RIGBY
Concert and exhibition
sponsored by *The Observer*
Lighting HARRY THOMAS
Television sound JEFF BAKER
Producer HUMPHREY BURTON
For the best effect, viewers
with stereo Radio 3 should
turn off tv sound and position their speakers on either
side of the screen, but a
few feet away. Stereo head-
phones are an alternative.

Radio Times,
29 March 1982.

Andre Previn:
BBC 1 10.40 pm

☐ **OMNIBUS**
(B.B.C.1, 10.40 p.m.)

"OMNIBUS" has moved to Wednesday just for "Walton No 1" which commemorates the 75th birthday of Sir William Walton. The main part of the programme is devoted to the rehearsal of Walton's First Symphony, which he wrote at 33.

André Previn conducts the London Symphony Orchestra and gives a detailed insight into the symphony's delights and complexities, which Previn calls "definitely one of those Desert Island Discs." There is also a filmed interview with the composer at his beautiful home on the Italian island of Ischia.

Daily Express, 23 March 1977. Previn rehearsed sections of the First Symphony. The complete performance televised by BBC-2 the following Sunday (director, Rodney Greenberg) featured a controversial innovation: for each movement of the symphony the orchestra was bathed in a different coloured light.

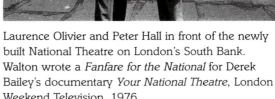

Scoring a birthday hit

TONIGHT'S CHOICE by Rosalie Horner

AT
THE HAUNTED END
OF THE DAY...
A PROFILE OF SIR WILLIAM WALTON
London Weekend Television

Brochure for Tony Palmer's 1981 film, which later won the Prix Italia and has been seen in more than thirty countries.

Walton in costume as the King of Saxony, a cameo role in Tony Palmer's epic *Wagner*, 1982. It was Walton's last appearance on camera.

The Royal Festival Hall, London, March 1977. Walton acknowledges the applause at his 75th birthday concert.

March 1977, a 75th birthday kiss from Susana. A course of acupuncture had helped Walton to recover from his collapse after *Troilus and Cressida*.

Green Room, Royal Festival Hall. Sir Georg Solti with Walton, after conducting *Belshazzar's Feast* with the London Philharmonic Orchestra.

Richard Baker, broadcaster. In 1977 he recited the first performance of some previously unpublished *Façade* numbers. He is one of the most accomplished speakers of the Sitwell poems, often sharing the platform with the composer's widow.

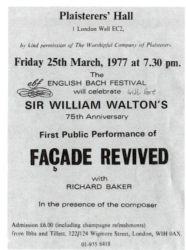

Façade Revived. The poems included "The Octogenarian" and "Said King Pompey". Four of the eight were later dropped by Walton in favour of other "leftovers rehashed" before publication in 1979 as *Façade 2*.

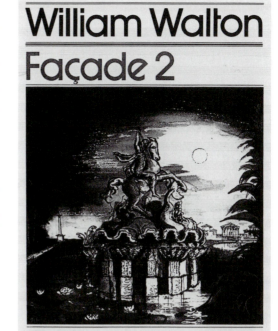

Façade 2. It was first heard at the 1979 Aldeburgh Festival. Peter Pears recited, with Steuart Bedford conducting.

Walton with the American singer Cathy Berberian, renowned for her vocal virtuosity. She performed *Façade* with great success at the 50th ISCM Festival in Siena, 1978. Walton was impressed and dedicated *Façade 2* to her.

Walton at the time of the First Symphony.

Walton loathed growing old. Comparison with the vitality of his youth was particularly painful. All too often he saw himself as

". . . getting gaga and incapacitated. I don't like it."

"I keep hoping that the Sinf. III will somehow materialise, but it shows little sign of doing so."

Royal Festival Hall, 20 February 1982. Walton with Mstislav Rostropovich at a rehearsal for the *Prologo e Fantasia*. They had met at the Aldeburgh Festival several years before. Such was Rostropovich's stature that Walton was persuaded to write not one but two works for him, one for solo cello and the other for his Washington orchestra.

Rostropovich was the leading cellist of his generation. When they first met, Walton urged him to take up his Cello Concerto. The cellist made a deal: "You write me new work, and I will play new work and old work." Walton composed a *Passacaglia for Solo Cello*; unfortunately he died before Rostropovich had an opportunity to play the Concerto.

LPO concert programme, 16 March 1982.

The Manuscript of *Prologo e Fantasia*. Walton worked on it for over a year. "I'm desperate to find a tune – if I do the OUP must pay me double royalties."

Programme for the première of *Prologo e Fantasia*. Walton was reassured when Rostropovich told him that the work was "full of vigour and sounded as if it had been written by a young man".

WILLIAM
WALTON
1902
1982
80th Birthday

Car sticker for Walton's 80th birthday.

The newly-opened Barbican Centre, London, March 1982. Left to right: Mark Elder (conductor), Sir Edward Heath, Walton, John Amis (interviewer), Nobuko Imai (viola soloist), Gillian Widdicombe (Arts Editor, *The Observer*), Norah Donnelly (sister), Susana.

Walton in a wheelchair at the Royal Festival Hall exhibition of his life and work curated by Gillian Widdicombe.

William and Susana
on the terrace of
La Mortella, 1981.

Walton's work-desk, photographed on the day of his death. The manuscript is his *Varii Capricci*. He had completed his revisions of the orchestral score only two days earlier.

The nine-bar coda of *Varii Capricci*.

Walton completed ballet score just before his death

By *AUGUSTUS TILLEY*

SIR WILLIAM WALTON, who has died aged 80 at his Ischia home where he had lived for more than 30 years, was once the *enfant terrible* of English music. Fame came to him at an unusually early age and he remained a leading English composer for fully 60 years.

Only last Sunday he completed the final bars of his score to the ballet version of "Varii Capricci," an orchestral work first performed in 1976. His publishers, Oxford University Press, received the manuscript on the day of his death.

Daily Telegraph, 6 March 1983.

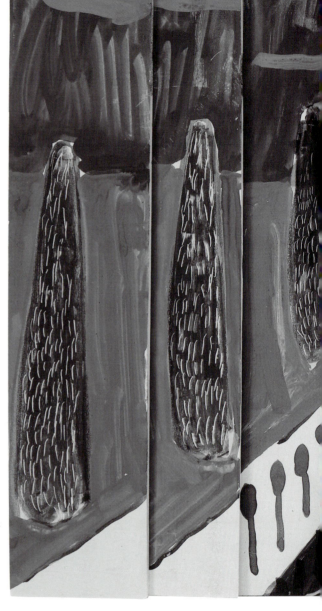

Anthony Dowell as Lo Straniero and Antoinette Sibley as La Capricciosa in the Royal Ballet's *Varii Capricci*, first performed at the Metropolitan Opera House, New York on 19 April 1983. The ballet was choreographed by Frederick Ashton, who dedicated it to "the memory of my lifelong friend". The ballet is set in the gardens of La Mortella. Scenery was by David Hockney and costumes by Ossie Clark.

Memorial plaque in Westminster Abbey, the gift of the Performing Right Society.

"William's Rock"
La Mortella, Ischia.

WILLIAM WALTON O.M.
1902 ~ 1983
SING A SONG OF PRAISE
BELOVED AND REVERED MASTER
THIS ROCK HOLDS HIS ASHES
THE GARDEN HE SURVEYS
RUSSELL PAGE DESIGNED
TOGETHER WE HAPPILY
BROUGHT IT TO LIFE
SUSANA

'ALL BLISS CONSISTS
IN THIS
TO DO AS ADAM DID.,
TRAHERNE 1637 - 1674

SELECTED COMPOSITIONS

Walton's major works are here listed alphabetically, by category with year of first performance. Other works mentioned in this book are also listed. The page numbers after each entry identify the references in the text.

For the complete list of Walton's compositions see Stewart Craggs, William Walton: A Catalogue, 2nd edition (Clarendon Press, 1990).

BALLET MUSIC:

(All works choreographed by Frederick Ashton)

Façade (1931) [p.43, 65, 76, 77]

First Shoot, The (1935) [p.65, 78]

Quest, The (1943) [p. 86, 92, 93]

Varii Capricci (1983) [p.157, 171, 172]

Wise Virgins, The (1940)
Music by J.S. Bach, orchestrated by Walton [p.86, 92]

CHAMBER MUSIC:

Quartet for Piano and Strings (published 1924) [p. 22, 23, 53]

Sonata for Violin and Piano (1949) [p.87, 105, 111]

String Quartet No. 1 (1923) [p.43, 52, 53]

String Quartet No. 2 in A Minor (1947) [p.86, 87, 100]

Variations for Violin and Piano on a Chorale by J.S. Bach (composed 1914) (manuscript lost) [p.20]

CHORAL MUSIC:

Belshazzar's Feast (1931)
Oratorio for Baritone, Mixed Chorus and Orchestra
Text selected from the Old Testament by Osbert Sitwell
[p.4, 13, 15, 32, 45, 62, 63, 66, 67, 105, 129, 140, 154, 165]

Cantico del Sole (1974)
Motet for unaccompanied Mixed Chorus (S.A.T.B.)
Text: St Francis of Assisi
[p.154]

Choral Fantasia (1916)
For Organ [p.20, 25]

Coronation Te Deum (1953)
For two Mixed Choruses, two Semi-Choruses, Boys' Voices, Organ, Orchestra and Military Brass [p.107,114]

Gloria (1961)
For Contralto, Tenor and Bass Soloists, Mixed Chorus and Orchestra [p.129,136]

In Honour of the City of London (1937)
Cantata for Mixed Chorus and Orchestra
Text: William Dunbar [p.65, 81]

Jubilate Deo (1972)
For Double Mixed Chorus and Organ

Litany, A (1916)
Partsong for unaccompanied Mixed Chorus
Text: Phineas Fletcher
[p.20, 26]

Magnificat and Nunc Dimittis (1975)
For Mixed Chorus and Organ

Set Me as a Seal Upon Thine Heart (1938)
Anthem for unaccompanied Mixed Chorus
Text: Song of Solomon

Twelve, The (1965)
Anthem for Mixed Chorus and Organ or Orchestra
Text: W.H. Auden
[p.130, 143]

Where Does the Uttered Music Go? (1946)
Motet for unaccompanied Mixed Chorus
Text: "Sir Henry Wood" by John Masefield
[p.86, 97

FILM MUSIC:

As You Like It (1936) [p.65, 79]
Other versions include:
Suite arranged by Carl Davis (1986)

Battle of Britain, The (1969)
[p.110, 131, 148, 149]
Other versions include:
Suite adapted by Colin Matthews (1985)

Dreaming Lips (1937) [p.65, 79]

Escape Me Never (1935) [p.53, 64, 79]
Other versions include:
Ballet Music arranged by the composer for Solo Piano

First of the Few, The (1942) [p.86, 89]
Other versions include:
Prelude and Fugue ("The Spitfire") transcribed by the composer

Foreman Went to France, The (1942)
[p.86, 89]

Hamlet (1948) [p. 87, 99]
Other versions include:
Hamlet: A Shakespeare Scenario.
Arranged by Christopher Palmer for Speaker and Orchestra (1989)

Henry V (1944) [p.86, 94, 95]
Other versions include:
Henry V: A Shakespeare Scenario.
Arranged by Christopher Palmer for Speaker, Mixed Chorus, Boys' Choir and Orchestra (1990)

Major Barbara (1941) [p.86, 89]

Next of Kin, The (1942) [p.86, 89]

Richard III (1955) [p.126, 132]
Other versions include:
Richard III: A Shakespeare Scenario.
Arranged by Christopher Palmer for Speaker and Orchestra

Stolen Life, A (1938) [p.65, 79]

Three Sisters (1970) [p.131, 149]

Went The Day Well? (1942) [p.86, 89]

MISCELLANEOUS:

Boy David, The (1936)
Incidental Music for J.M. Barrie's play [p.79]

Choral Prelude on "Wheatley" (1916)
For Organ (unpublished) [p.27]

Christopher Columbus (1942)
Incidental Music for the radio play by

Louis MacNeice [p.86, 91]
Other versions include:
Cantata for Contralto, Tenor, Baritone, Mixed Chorus and Orchestra devised by Carl Davis (2002)

Duets for Children (1940)
Ten pieces for Piano Duet [p.7, 86]

Façade (1922)
An Entertainment for Reciter and Instrumentalists
Text: Poems by Edith Sitwell
Façade was frequently revised with new numbers added and others dropped. The definitive selection of 21 numbers was not published until 1951.
[p.4, 10, 11, 42, 43, 45, 48, 49, 50, 63, 98, 100, 105, 112, 162, 165]

Façade 2: A Further Entertainment (1979)
[p.165]

Fanfare for The National (1976) [p.163]

First Shoot, The (1980)
Arranged by the composer for Brass Band [p.13, 156]

Five Bagatelles for Guitar (1971)
[p.131, 151]

Granada TV Prelude (1965)
Arranged by Gilbert Vinter for Symphonic Wind Band [p.162]

Macbeth (1942)
Incidental Music for John Gielgud's stage production [p.86, 90, 91]

Passacaglia for Solo Cello (1982)
[p.156, 168]

Son of Heaven, The (1925)
Incidental Music for Lytton Strachey's play
[p.44, 54]

Valse in C Minor (1917)
For Solo Piano (unpublished) [p.31]

OPERAS:

Bear, The (1967)
Extravaganza in One Act
Libretto by Paul Dehn and Walton after Anton Chekhov [p.128, 130, 144, 145, 162]

Troilus and Cressida (1954)
Opera in Three Acts
Libretto by Christopher Hassall
[p.87, 98, 101, 106, 107, 113, 116–24, 126, 128, 129, 155, 156, 161, 164]

ORCHESTRAL MUSIC:

Capriccio Burlesco (1968) [p.130, 147]

Concerto for Viola and Orchestra (1929) [p.4, 15, 62, 64, 65, 147, 154]

Concerto for Violin and Orchestra (1939) [p.4, 65, 82, 83, 88, 147]

Concerto for Violoncello and Orchestra (1957) [p.4, 126, 127, 132, 133]

Crown Imperial (1937) [p.65, 80, 81, 107]

Dr. Syntax (unperformed: manuscript missing) [p.44, 46]

Façade Suite No. 1 (1926) [p.43, 54]

Façade Suite No. 2 (1938) [p.43]

Fantasia Concertante (unperformed: manuscript missing) [p.44, 51]

Improvisations on an Impromptu by Benjamin Britten (1970) [p.128, 146]

Johannesburg Festival Overture (1956) [p.126]

Music for Children (1941)

Orb and Sceptre (1953) [p.107, 114]

Partita for Orchestra (1958) [p.127, 134]

Portsmouth Point (1926) [p.44, 55]

Prelude for Orchestra (1977) [p.162]

Prologo e Fantasia (1982) [p.156, 168]

Scapino (1941) [p.86, 90, 91]

Siesta (1926) [p.45, 56]

Sinfonia Concertante for Orchestra with Piano Obbligato (1928) [p.45, 58, 59]

Sonata for Strings (1972)
Transcription for String Orchestra of *String Quartet No. 2 in A Minor*

Symphony No. 1 (1935) [p.63–65, 70–75, 129, 131, 150, 156, 163, 166]

Symphony No. 2 (1960) [p.127, 135]
Symphony No. 3 (unfinished)
[p.154, 160, 167]

Variations on a Theme by Hindemith (1963) [p.128, 142]

Varii Capricci (1976)
Orchestral transcription of *Five Bagatelles for Guitar* [p.131]

Wise Virgins, The (1940)
Music by J.S. Bach arranged by Walton

VOCAL MUSIC:

Anon in Love (1959)
Song Cycle for Tenor and Guitar.
Text: Anon. 16th & 17th century poems selected by Christopher Hassall
[p.128, 134]
Re-scored for Tenor and Small Orchestra (1971)

Song for the Lord Mayor's Table, A (1962)
Song Cycle for Soprano and Piano
Poems by William Blake, Thomas Jordan, Charles Morris, William Wordsworth and Anon selected by Christopher Hassall
[p.130]

Tell Me Where is Fancy Bred? (composed 1916)
Song for Soprano and tenor voices,
3 Violins and Piano (unpublished)
Text by William Shakespeare [p.20]

Three Songs (1932)
"Daphne", "Through Gilded Trellises" and "Old Sir Faulk"
Poems by Edith Sitwell [p.55]

Winds, The (1921)
Song for Voice and Piano
Text: A.C. Swinburne [p.38]

WILLIAM WALTON EDITION
David Lloyd-Jones, General Editor.

Oxford University Press have undertaken the ambitious project of publishing a William Walton Edition in twenty-three newly-set hardback volumes.
Four have already been published: Symphony No. 1, Shorter Choral Works, Façade and Henry V: A Shakespeare Scenario. Most of the other volumes are in active preparation. They are listed below:

Stage Works
Volume 1 Troilus and Cressida
Volume 2 The Bear
Volume 3 Ballets

Choral Works
Volume 4 Belshazzar's Feast
Volume 5 Choral Works with Orchestra
Volume 6 Shorter Choral Works without Orchestra

Vocal Works
Volume 7 Façade Entertainments
Volume 8 Vocal Music

Orchestral Music
Volume 9 Symphony No. 1
Volume 10 Symphony No. 2
Volume 11 Sinfonia Concertante (original and revised versions)
Volume 12 Viola Concerto (original and revised versions)
Volume 13 Violin Concerto and Cello Concerto
Volume 14 Overtures
Volume 15 Orchestral Works – 1
Volume 16 Orchestral Works – 2
Volume 17 Shorter Orchestral Works – 1
Volume 18 Shorter Orchestral Works – 2

Chamber Music
Volume 19 Chamber Music

Instrumental Music
Volume 20 Instrumental Music

Music for Brass
Volume 21 Music for Brass

Film Music
Volume 22 Shakespeare Film Suites
Volume 23 Henry V: A Shakespeare Scenario

David Lloyd-Jones writes: "the William Walton Edition will ensure that this composer's ever-increasing popularity at the start of the twenty-first century will be complemented by performing material which is edited to the highest contemporary standards and which, at the same time, is eminently practical. The editions will also include carefully researched introductory essays and extensive critical notes."

SELECTED BIBLIOGRAPHY

BIOGRAPHIES OF WILLIAM WALTON:

CRAGGS Stewart, *William Walton, A Catalogue*, 2nd edition (Clarendon Press, 1990)

CRAGGS Stewart, *William Walton. A Source Book* (Scolar Press, 1993)

HAYES Malcolm (Editor), *Selected Letters of William Walton* (Faber & Faber, 2001)

KENNEDY Michael, *Portrait of Walton* (OUP, 1989)

LLOYD Stephen, *William Walton: Muse of Fire*, (Boydell and Brewer, 2000)

OTTAWAY Hugh, *Walton. Novello Short Biographies* (Sevenoaks, 1972)

PALMER Tony, *At the Haunted End of the Day* (© Ladbroke Films Ltd, 1981)

TIERNEY Neil, *William Walton: His Life and Music* (Hale, 1984)

WALTON Susana, *William Walton: Behind The Façade* (OUP, 1987)

OTHER WORKS:

ABERCONWAY Christabel, *A Wiser Woman?* (Hutchinson, 1966)

AMORY Mark, *Lord Berners: The Last Eccentric* (Chatto & Windus, 1998)

BEATON Cecil, *Diaries: The Wandering Years, 1922–39* (Weidenfeld & Nicolson, 1961)

BRADFORD Sarah, *Sacheverell Sitwell* (Sinclair Stevenson, 1993)

BROWN Jane, *Lutyens and the Edwardians* (Viking, 1996)

BURTON Humphrey, *Menuhin* (Faber & Faber Ltd, 2000)

CAMPBELL Roy, *Light on a Dark Horse* (Hollis & Carter, 1951)

COCHRAN Charles B., *The Secrets of a Showman* (William Heinemann Ltd, 1929)

COCHRAN Charles B., *Cock-A-Doodle-Do* (J.M. Dent & Sons Ltd, 1941)

FARNAN Dorothy J., *Auden in Love* (Faber & Faber Ltd, 1985)

FONTEYN Margot, *Autobiography* (W.H. Allen & Co Ltd, 1975)

GARAFOLA Lynn, *Diaghilev's Ballets Russes* (OUP, 1989)

GATHORNE HARDY Robert (Ed.), *Ottoline at Garsington* (Faber & Faber Ltd, 1974)

GLENDINNING Victoria, *A Unicorn Among Lions* (Weidenfeld & Nicolson, 1981)

GRAY Cecil, *Musical Chairs, or Between Two Stools* (Home & van Thal, 1948)

GROVE *The New Dictionary Of Music and Musicians* (Macmillan & Co, 1980)

HART-DAVIS Rupert (Ed.), *Diaries of Siegfried Sassoon, 1920–25* (Faber & Faber Ltd, 1981)

HEATH Edward, *Music – A Joy for Life* (Sidgwick & Jackon, 1976)

HINNELLS Duncan, *An Extraordinary Performance* (OUP, 1998)

HOARE Philip, *Serious Pleasures: The Life of Stephen Tennant* (Hamish Hamilton, 1990)

HOWES Frank, *The Music of William Walton* (OUP, 1965)

HUGHES Patrick (Spike), *Opening Bars* (Pilot Press, 1946)

KAVANAGH Julie, *Secret Muses* (Faber & Faber Ltd, 1996)

KING Viva, *The Weeping and the Laughter* (Macdonald & Jane's, 1976)

LAMBERT Constant, *Music, Ho! A Study of Music in Decline* (Faber and Faber Ltd, 1934)

LEHMANN John, *A Nest of Tigers: Edith, Osbert and Sacheverell Sitwell in their Times* (Macmillan & Co, 1968)

LUTYENS Elizabeth, *A Goldfish Bowl* (Cassell & Co Ltd, 1972)

MAINE Basil, *Twang with our Music* (The Epworth Press, 1957)

McCABE John, *Alan Rawsthorne: Portrait of a Composer* (OUP, 1999)

MIDDLETON James, *Oldham, Past and Present* (Edwards & Bryning Ltd, 1903)

MITCHELL Donald & REED Philip, *Letters from a Life: Selected Letters and Diaries of Benjamin Britten* (Faber & Faber Ltd, 1991 2 Vols.)

MOORCROFT-WILSON Jean, *Siegfried Sassoon: The Making of a War Poet* (Duckworth, 1998)

MOTION Andrew, *The Lamberts* (The Hogarth Press, 1987)

NEWTON Ivor, *At The Piano: The World of an Accompanist* (Hamish Hamilton, 1966)

NICHOLS Beverly, *The Sweet and Twenties* (Weidenfeld & Nicolson, 1958)

OSBORNE Charles, *W. H. Auden: The Life of a Poet* (Eyre Methuen, 1980)

PALMER Tony, *A Life On The Road* (Macdonald & Co Ltd, 1982)

PEARSON John, *Façades: Edith, Osbert and Sacheverell Sitwell* (Macmillan & Co Ltd, 1978)

SECREST Meryle, *Kenneth Clark: A Biography* (Weidenfeld & Nicolson, 1984)

SHEAD Richard, *Constant Lambert* (Simon Publications, Lutterworth Press, 1973)

SITWELL Edith, *Taken Care Of* (Hutchinson & Co Ltd, 1965)

SITWELL Edith, *Selected Letters* (Macmillan & Co Ltd, 1970)

SITWELL Osbert, *Argonaut and Juggernaut* (Chatto & Windus, 1919)

SITWELL Osbert, *Laughter in the Next Room* (Macmillan & Co Ltd, 1949)

SKELTON Geoffrey, *Paul Hindemith: The Man Behind the Music* (Victor Gollancz Ltd, 1975)

SKIPWITH Joanna (Ed.), *The Sitwells and the Arts of the 1920s and 1930s* (National Portrait Gallery Publications, 1994)

STUART ROBERTS John, *Siegfried Sassoon* (Richard Cohen Books, 1999)

TERTIS Lionel, *My Viola and I* (Paul Elek Ltd, 1974)

TILLIS Malcolm, *Chords & Discords: The Life of an Orchestral Musician* (Phoenix House, 1960)

TOVEY Donald Francis, *Essays In Musical Analysis* (OUP, 1936)

VAUGHAN David, *Frederick Ashton and his Ballets* (A. & C. Black Ltd, 1974)

VICKERS Hugo, *Cecil Beaton* (Weidenfeld & Nicolson, 1985)

ZIEGLER Philip, *Osbert Sitwell* (Chatto, 1998)

RECORDINGS OF WALTON'S MUSIC

Apart from *The Wise Virgins* (his Ballet Suite arranged from music by J.S. Bach), Walton conducted only his own music for recordings. His first venture into the field was at the Chenil Galleries, London, in 1929, when he conducted eleven numbers from *Façade*. Over the next forty years he made 78s and then LPs of most of his compositions. Many of those recordings are now available on CD. He died just as the modern era of digital recording was emerging, but new versions of his major works, notably the concertos, continue to be released. The outstanding venture in this field is the complete edition produced by Chandos Records (http://www.chandos.net). EMI produced a remastered collection in a set of three CDs in the 1990s. For the latest information consult the William Walton website at: http://www.waltontrust.org.uk

AUTHORS' ACKNOWLEDGEMENTS

In addition to the help from Stuart Craggs, Michael Kennedy and Lady Walton referred to in their Preface, the authors also wish to thank:

Heather Aalstrom of the Houghton Library, Harvard University
Pauline Allwright and Joanne Ratcliffe of the Imperial War Museum
Mark Amory
Caroline Annesley
Michael Aston
Derek Bailey
Simon Bailey and Polly Smith of Oxford University Archives
Nick Baker of Eton College
Chris Barwick and the staff of the Hulton Getty Picture Collection
Susanne Baumgartner of the Estate of Lord Menuhin
Caroline Belgrave of Curtis Brown
Terry Berry and the staff of Oldham Local Studies Library
John Bodley
Elizabeth Briggs of the West Yorkshire Archive Service
David Buchanan of Wood End Museum, Scarborough
Christina Burton
The Rt. Hon. Sir Adam Butler
Kate Calloway of EMI Archives
Norma Campbell Vickers
Paul Carr
Vivien Cartwright and the staff of Leeds Local Studies Library
Alastair Chisholm
Jessica Chitty of the National Gallery
Jane Clark
Paul Collen of the Royal College of Music
Frances Cook of the London Philharmonic Orchestra
Fiona Cowan
Jennifer Cozens, James Kilvington and the staff of the National Portrait Gallery
Lydia Cresswell Jones
Judith Curthoys and the staff of Christ Church College Library
Caroline Dalton of New College, Oxford
Patricia Daly of *The Dancing Times*
Sue Daly and the staff of Sotheby's Picture Library
Giles Dalziel Smith

John Denison CBE
Martin Denny
Carol Djukanovic
Dr Jenny Doctor and Kieron Cooke of The Britten-Pears Library
Claire Doherty
Roy Douglas
Martin Durrant of the V&A Picture Library
Nicholas Edgar of Rosenstiel's
Jonathan Edmunds of New College School
Robert Edwards
David Farrell
Diana Foss-Sparkes
Peter Fox of Oldham Museum
Francesca Franchi, Robert Woodward and the staff of the Archives of the Royal Opera House, Covent Garden
Donald Garstang of P&D Colnaghi & Co Ltd
Andrea Gieseke of Schott-Mainz
Vincent Giroud and the staff of the Beinecke Rare Book and Manuscript Library, Yale University
Christopher Glass
Graham Glen of *Nottingham Evening Post*
Jim Godfrey
Jill Gomez
Adrian Goodman
Philip Goodman
Sally Groves and Rachel Oakley of Schott Music Publishers
The Hon. Julian Guest
Patricia Hauck of The Courier-Journal, Louisville, Kentucky
Barbara Hawes, Richard Wandel and Michele Smith of New York Philharmonic Archives
Philip Hoare
David Hockney and the staff of the David Hockney Studio
Helen Hogan
Megan Hollingshead of New York City Opera
Hannah Holm
Prue Hopkins
Diane Hudson of the Fitzwilliam Museum, Cambridge
Charmian Hughes
Roger Hughes of Radio Times
Jeremy Hulme of Faringdon House
John Huntley

Peter Hutton
Carol Jacobs of the Cleveland Orchestra Archives
Tim Jacques
Lin Jammet of the Frink Estate
Natalie Jones of Katz Pictures
The staff of the Kensington & Chelsea Central Library
John-Paul Kernot of the Bill Brandt Archive
Tim Kerr of PA Photos
Anthony Kersting
Frederick R. Koch
Nina Large of EMI Classics
Elbie Lebrecht
Keith Lee of Helen Bradley Prints
Elizabeth Levanti of the Carnegie Museum of Art, Pittsburgh
Clarissa Lewis
Kori Lockhart of San Francisco Opera
Godfrey MacDomnic
Sarah Maddock of Penguin Books
Richard Mangan of the Raymond Mander and Joe Mitchenson Theatre Collection
Penny McGuire of London Weekend Television
The Hon. Christopher McLaren
Michael McLaren
Daniel Meadows
Prof. Edward Mendelson
James Merifield
Chris Merka-Richards of the British Museum
Polly Miller of EMI Records
Bobbie Mitchell and the staff of the BBC Photograph Library
Jean Moorcroft-Wilson
Wyn Morris
George Mott
Margaret de Motte of the Local Studies Unit, Manchester Central Library
Alan Mottram and Fiona Carnan of Christ Church Cathedral School
Tony Palmer
Sofka Papadimitrou
Reale Patalano
Iris Pfeiffer of the Arnold Schoenberg Center
Patricia Pince van der Aa of the Maria Austria Instituut
Richard Pitkin of Illustrated London News
Andrew Plant

Dr Omar S. Pound
Sir André Previn
Jane Pritchard of Rambert Dance Company
Enzo Rando
Dr Shirley Rodden of The Courtauld Institute
Tony Russell
Enar Merkel Rydberg
Peter Sargent
Luitgard Schader of the Paul-Hindemith-Institut
Susan Scott and The Savoy Group
Francis Sitwell
Sir Reresby Sitwell Bt, DL
Mike Smith
Elisabeth Söderström
Lady Solti
Ivor Spencer-Thomas
Lady Natasha Spender
Clive Strutt
Terence Taylour
Martin Thacker of the Henry Watson Music Library
The staff of the Theatre Museum, London
Janet Tod of D.A.C.S.
Jack Vartoogian
Ursula Vaughan Williams
Nuala la Vertue of the Centre for Oxfordshire Studies
Keith Wakefield of Stainer & Bell Ltd
Christopher Warde-Jones
Dr John Warrack
Tony Watson of *The Yorkshire Post*
Andy Webb and the staff of the Kobal Collection
Gillian Widdicombe
Jim Williams of Oldham Chronicle
Stephannie Williams
Rosemary Williamson of the Royal Northern College of Music
Reg Wilson
Viscount Wimborne
Dave Withey of Finsbury Library
Tana Wollen and the staff of the National Film Archive
Dr Susan Wollenberg of University of Oxford Faculty of Music
David Wright, Beverley Cole and the staff of the National Railway Museum
Valerie Zars of Getty-Liaison
Carola Zogolovitch

PICTURE CREDITS

The following abbreviations are used throughout:

ATHEOTD (*At the Haunted End of the Day* © Ladbroke Films Ltd)
BFI (BFI Films, Stills, Posters & Designs)
BRA (Ballet Rambert Archive)
CCCS (Christ Church Cathedral School)
FRKC (The Frederick R. Koch Collection of the Beinecke Rare Book & Manuscript Library, Yale University)
GBCCO (The Governing Body of Christ Church, Oxford)
ILN (Illustrated London News Picture Library)
IWM (Imperial War Museum, London)
M&M (The Mander & Mitchenson Theatre Collection)
NFA (National Film Archive)
NPG (National Portrait Gallery, London)
OCCPA (Oxfordshire County Council Photographic Archive)
OLS (Oldham Local Studies Library)
OUP (Oxford University Press)
RCM (Royal College of Music, London)
SPL (Sotheby's Picture Library, London)
V&A (Victoria & Albert Museum – Picture Library)
WWA (William Walton Archive, Ischia)

TITLE PAGE

Photograph by Arnold Newman. (© Arnold Newman/Liaison Agency)

CHAPTER 1: THE OLDHAM CHILDHOOD (1902–1912)

PAGE 1
Oldham Market Place. From: *Oldham In Old Photographs* by Eric Krieger. (OLS)

PAGES 2 & 3
Cotton Spinners. (OLS)
Mr & Mrs Charles Walton. (WWA)

PAGE 4 & 5
Top of High Street, Oldham. From: *Oldham As It Was* by John Stafford. (OLS)
Oldham Belles. From: *Oldham Past* by Cliff Hayes. (OLS)

PAGES 6 & 7
The Turner Family Tree. (WWA)
Charles Walton. Photograph by Jas. Bacon & Sons, Leeds. (WWA)
Louie Turner. Photograph by A. Whitla, The Oxford Portrait Studio, Manchester. (WWA)
Turner-Walton wedding group. (WWA)
Walton and his brother Noel. Photograph by Dyson, Oldham. (WWA)
Walton's registry of birth certificate. (WWA)

PAGES 8 & 9
Werneth postcard. (OLS)
Map of Oldham, 1902. (OLS)
Platt Brothers' Hartford New Works. (OLS)
Walton and Noel outside 93 Werneth Hall Road. (WWA)
Werneth Board School. (OLS)
Walton and Noel as choirboys. (WWA)
St John's Church interior. (ATHEOTD)
St John's Church exterior. From: *A Brief History Of St. John's* by The Rev. W. A. Westley, B.A. (OLS)

PAGES 10 & 11
Walton & Noel in sailor suits. (WWA)
Oldham Wakes Fair. (OLS)
Blackpool & Lytham poster. (OLS)
Walton's first letter to mother. (WWA)
Family at the seaside circa 1910. (OLS)
"Blackpool Station". Painting by Helen Bradley. (By kind permission of Helen Bradley Prints)

PAGES 12 & 13
"Whit Sunday". Painting by Helen Bradley. (By kind permission of Helen Bradley Prints)
Beautiful Oldham Society. Bookplate by N. Strain. (Oldham Museum)
Werneth Park Flower Show Day. From: *Beautiful Oldham Society – A Record 1902–1912.* (OLS)
Smallwood's Piano Tutor. (Publ. by: Francis Day & Hunter Ltd. Courtesy of Mrs P. Ashcroft)
Fancy Dress Cycle Parade, 1908. (OLS)
Mr Granelli & his ice cream cart. (OLS)

PAGES 14 & 15
Oldham Orchestral Society at Greenacres Hall, Oldham. From: *Oldham Orchestral Society Programmes 1902–1904.* (Oldham Museum)
Oldham Orchestral Society programme, 23 February 1912. From: *Oldham Orchestral Society Programmes 1901–1926.* (Oldham Museum)
Manchester Free Trade Hall. (Archives & Local Studies, Manchester Libraries Central Library)
Boris Godounov programme. (Courtesy of The Director, Manchester Libraries and Theatres)
Sir Thomas Beecham. Photograph by H. Walter Barnett. (V&A)

PAGES 16 & 17
Various Oldham hostelries. (OLS)
Fruiterer's Shop, Oldham. From: *Oldham In Old Photographs* by Eric Krieger. (OLS)
Advertisement for choristers. *Manchester Guardian*, 11 May 1912.

PAGE 18
Walton and mother in railway carriage. (ATHEOTD)
Railway ticket. (Courtesy of National Railway Museum, York)

CHAPTER 2: A SUPERIOR EDUCATION (1912–1920)

PAGE 19
Walton as a schoolboy. (WWA)
St Aldate's Front, Christ Church. Valentine Series postcard. (By kind permission of GBCCO)
"O Lord our Governor". (WWA)

PAGES 20 & 21
Christ Church Cathedral School. Drawing by D. J. Godfrey.
Choirboys' toothbrushes and socks. Photograph by Humphrey Burton.

PAGES 24 & 25
CCCS class of 1912. (WWA)
Walton's letter to mother, 17 November 1912. (WWA)
Choirboys entering the choir school. (ATHEOTD)
CCCS Magazine, January 1913. (WWA)
Sir Hugh Allen, Varley Roberts & Henry Ley. Postcard photograph by E.E. Turner of Oxford. (© RCM)
Dr T.B. Strong. Photograph by Lafayette. (NPG)

PAGES 26 & 27
The King's Visit To Oxford. (Courtesy of OCCPA)
A Litany Holograph Mss. (Courtesy of FRKC)
Royal Flying Corps in Peckwater Quad, Christ Church College. (IWM Neg. No. Q30.264)
Wounded soldiers in wheelchairs. (IWM Neg. No. Q30.282)
Aeroplane flight. (Courtesy of OCCPA)
Walton's letter to mother, 10 September 1916. (WWA)
Choral Prelude on Wheatley Holograph Mss. (Courtesy of Manuscript Collections The British Library [Reference Division] Add. MS 52384)
CCCS Prizegiving Programme, 3 November 1916. (WWA)

PAGES 28 & 29
"When you're a long, long way from home" postcard. (Oldham Museum. Lyrics reproduced by kind permission of Francis Day & Hunter)
Still from *The Battle of the Somme*. (IWM Neg. Ref. Q70169)
Walton's letters to mother. (WWA)

PAGES 30 & 31
Sir Hubert Parry. Photograph by E. O. Hoppe. (Mansell/Time Inc/Katz)
Walton's letter to mother, 24 June 1917. (WWA)
Christ Church Cathedral interior. (By kind permission of GBCCO)
Walton's school report, 4 November 1917. (WWA)
Valse Holograph Mss. (By kind permission of Christ Church Library, Oxford)
The Radcliffe Camera. (Courtesy of OCCPA)
CCCS Prizegiving Programme, 9 November 1917. (WWA)
Extract from CCCS Headmaster's diary. (Courtesy of CCCS)

PAGES 32 & 33
"Belshazzar's Feast" by Rembrandt. (Reproduced by kind permission of The National Gallery, London)
Walton's letter to mother, 16 July 1918. (WWA)

Tom Quad, Christ Church, Oxford. (By kind permission of GBCCO)
Walton's letter to mother, 23 October 1918. (WWA)
Portrait of Roy Campbell by Augustus John [1878–1961]. (© Courtesy of the artist's estate/Bridgeman Art Library. Source: Carnegie Museum of Art, Pittsburgh; Patrons Art Fund)

PAGES 34 & 35
Christ Church 2nd Eight, 1919. (By kind permission of GBCCO)
Frank Prewett (detail). (By kind permission of GBCCO)
Oars and flags of Christ Church. (Courtesy of OCCPA)
Walton's letter to mother, 6 November 1918. (WWA)
Walton as cox with 2nd Eight Rowing Team, 1919. (Courtesy of Gillian Widdicombe)

PAGES 36 & 37
Portrait of Siegfried Sassoon by Glyn Philpot. (Fitzwilliam Museum, Cambridge)
D'Oyly Carte poster. (Courtesy of OCCPA)
Garsington Manor. (Courtesy of Philip Goodman)
Walton sitting cross-legged (detail). (By kind permission of GBCCO)
"Umbrellas" (The Garsington Set). Painting by Dorothy Brett. (© Reserved)
"Zverev and Lopokova loosening up before a performance of 'Parade' in London 1919" by Dame Laura Knight. (Reproduced with permission of Curtis Brown Ltd, London, on behalf of the Estate of Dame Laura Knight. © Dame Laura Knight)

PAGES 38 & 39
Sacheverell Sitwell. Photograph by Denys. (NPG)
Osbert Sitwell. Photograph by E.O. Hoppe. (Mansell/Time Inc/Katz)
Edith Sitwell. (© Hulton Getty)
"Dinner At The Golden Cross" by Gabriel Atkin. (Scarborough Art Gallery. Reproduced by kind permission of Sir Reresby Sitwell Bt DL)
Walton's letter to mother, 11 March 1919. (WWA)
Sir Hugh Allen. (© RCM)
Percy Carter Buck. (© RCM)
Ralph Vaughan Williams. Photograph by E.O. Hoppe. (Mansell/Time Inc/Katz)
Extract from Trinity Term 1920 Examination Register. (Oxford University Archives Ref: UR3/4/4/1)

PAGE 40
Walton's Record from the Oxford Examinations Register (1902–1920). (Oxford University Archives Ref: UR2/9/3)

CHAPTER 3: THE ARTFUL LODGER (1920–1929)

PAGE 41
Mr Cochran's Young Ladies. Photograph by Leadlay. (M&M)
Chorus Girls. (M&M)
More Chorus Girls. Photograph by Stage Photo Co. (M&M)
Walton as young man. Photograph by Cecil Beaton. (Courtesy of SPL)
"Satyr" decorative corners. (Archives of The Savoy Group)

PAGES 42 & 43
Frontispiece from "Façade", 1922 by Gino Severini. (© ADAGP, Paris and DACS, London 2000)

PAGES 44 & 45
Edith Sitwell, 1921 by Powys Evans. (SPL. Reproduced by kind permission of Terence Taylour)
Bust of William Walton by Maurice Lambert. Photograph by Christopher Warde-Jones.

PAGES 46 & 47
Walton at the piano. Photograph by Cecil Beaton. (Courtesy of SPL)
Edward Dent. Photograph by La Moderna, Bologna. (© RCM)
Ernest Ansermet. (© RCM)
Feruccio Busoni. Photograph by Siri Fischer-Schneevoigt, Verlag Herman Leiser, Berlin. (M&M)
Eugene Goossens. Photogravure by Herbert Lambert. (NPG)
2 Carlyle Square, Chelsea. Drawing by Tim Jacques.
Montegufoni. Photograph by Emery Walker. (NPG)

Albergo Cappuccini. (ATHEOTD)
"South For Winter Sunshine". Poster by Edmond Vaughan. (© National Railway Museum, York)

PAGES 48 & 49
Façade curtain by Frank Dobson. (WWA)
Programme for *Façade* at The Aeolian Hall, 12 June 1923. (RCM)
The Sitwells, Walton and Neil Porter. Photograph by Pacific & Atlantic Photos Ltd. (WWA)
"Metrics through the megaphone". *The Evening Standard*, 13 June 1923. (By permission of The British Library)
"Why Did They Do It?" (detail). Cartoon by Tom Titt. (*The Orbit*, October 1926)
"Poetry through a megaphone". *Daily Express*, 13 June 1923. (By permission of The British Library)
"Wonderful London Yesterday" / "Drivel They Paid To Hear" / "Fireman Tells The Truth". *The Daily Graphic*, 14 June 1923. (By permission of The British Library)
"Latest gossip of the London season". *The Sunday Express*, 17 June 1923. (By permission of The British Library)
Back room, ground floor 2 Carlyle Square (bowl with press cuttings). Photograph by E.J. Mason. (By permission of IPC Syndication)
The Swiss Family Whittlebot. Photograph by Stage Photo Co. (WWA)

PAGES 50 & 51
Debroy Somers "Savoy Medley". (Score publ. by Keith Prowse & Co Ltd)
Debroy Somers & The Savoy Orpheans, 1923. (Archives of The Savoy Group)
Florence Mills, 1923. (M&M)
Constant Lambert. Photograph by Yvonne Gregory. (NPG)
Musical note icons and musical dance frieze. From: *The Savoy Orpheans* publ. privately at The Savoy Hotel, 1924. (Archives of The Savoy Group)
Walton as a young man. Photograph by Cecil Beaton. (Courtesy of SPL)
The Orpheans in the Ballroom of The Savoy Hotel (shot through harp). From: *The Savoy Orpheans* publ. privately at The Savoy Hotel, 1924. (Archives of The Savoy Group)
"Dance Fervour At The Savoy". (Archives of The Savoy Group)
Paul Whiteman and his "jazz" Orchestra, 1923. (M&M)

PAGES 52 & 53
String Quartet No. 1 Mss (extract). (Courtesy of FRKC)
Alban Berg with Arnold Schoenberg's portrait of him. (Arnold Schoenberg Center, Vienna)
"Willie Walton 1925" by Christopher Wood. (WWA)
"Quartet". From: *Manchester Guardian*, 6 August 1923. (WWA)
Hyam Greenbaum. (Reproduction after a photograph by Maurice Beck & Helen MacGregor. © RCM)
Philip Heseltine. (© RCM)
Vladimir Dukelsky. From: *Programme for the International Society For Contemporary Music, Oxford, 1931.* (© RCM)
Quartet for Piano & Strings. Carnegie Collection of British Music. (Score publ. by Stainer & Bell Ltd)
George Gershwin. (M&M)
Bernard van Dieren. (Courtesy of Alistair Chisholm)
Angus Morrison. Photograph by Emil Otto Hoppe. (Katz Pictures Ltd. Courtesy of Mrs Elizabeth Panourgias)

PAGES 54 & 55
The Triumph of Neptune cast list. (WWA)
Lytton Strachey. From: *Ottoline At Garsington* ed. Robert Gathorne Hardy. (Publ. Faber & Faber 1974)
The Son Of Heaven cast list. (WWA)
Serge Diaghilev. (Lebrecht Collection)
Lord Berners with Serge Lifar & Alexandra Danilova. Photograph by Sasha, 1926. (V&A)
Walton & Hubert Foss. (By kind permission of Mrs Diana Foss Sparkes)
Portsmouth Point piano duet score. (Publ. by OUP)
Dora Stevens (Mrs Foss). (By kind permission of Mrs Diana Foss Sparkes)
"Portsmouth Point" by Thomas Rowlandson. (© Copyright The British Museum)